Down the Belliard Steps
Discovering the Brontës in Brussels

1

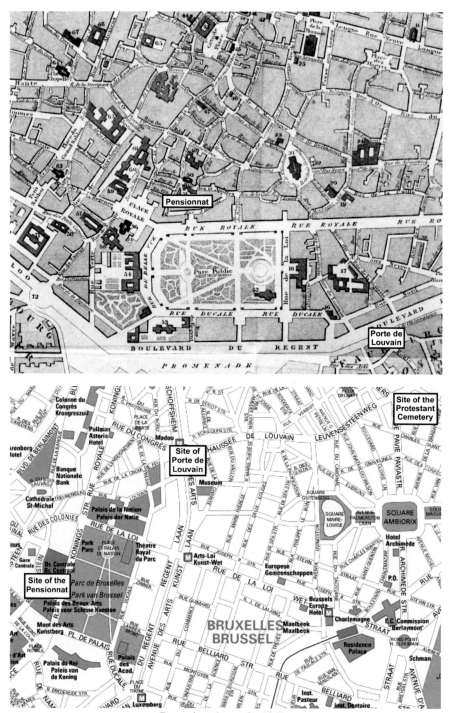

Brussels today and c.1840

Down the Belliard Steps
Discovering the Brontës in Brussels

Helen MacEwan

Brussels Brontë Editions

MMXII

Published by
Brussels Brontë Editions
Hythe, Kent.

First published 2012

ISBN 978-0-9573772-0-2

Cover photo:
The Belliard Steps or Passage de la Bibliothèque as it was then known, c. 1900
(*Dexia Bank postcard collection*)

Printed & bound in Great Britain by
The Blissett Group
London

Paper produced from wood grown in sustainable forests.

Contents

Acknowledgements

I would like to acknowledge my debt to Eric Ruijssenaars' *Charlotte Brontë's Promised Land: The Pensionnat and other Brontë places in Brussels*, which is evident throughout this book, particularly in the first chapters. I am also indebted to Eric for my title *Down the Belliard Steps*, which he used before me as the name of a lecture.

I am grateful to Brian Bracken, Paul Gretton, Maureen Peeck and Christine Went for reading through the manuscript and making suggestions, to Selina Busch for her help with the cover design and illustrations, to Marina Saegerman and Tanja Vanmeenen for cover design ideas, and to Jean Samuel for technical aspects.

This book recounts the projects and experiences of various members of the Brussels Brontë Group. I would like to thank them for making it possible by sharing those experiences with me, and dedicate the book to all those who have joined and supported the group over the years.

Foreword

For most Brontë enthusiasts, Brussels is the city where Charlotte and Emily went to study and which inspired two of Charlotte's novels. Few of them probably know much about Brussels today. For those not acquainted with the Belgian capital, the modern-day city may conjure up little more than a place where European Union summits are held and directives issued. This account of how a branch of the Brontë Society grew up in Brussels may provide glimpses of a different city and of what it is like to live and work here.

It is an account of a group of people brought together in their exploration of what is perhaps the least-known aspect of a much-written-about family – its two most famous members' Brussels adventure. It is the story of our own Brussels adventure, which was inspired by theirs.

Helen MacEwan
Brussels, 2012

Introduction

This is the story of an unusual literary association, a branch of the Brontë Society born in the strange capital city that is Brussels.

The Brontë Society has always been one of the most popular of the many associations that honour Britain's writers. The age of the Internet and Facebook has seen a decline in the numbers of members who gather in church halls to listen to talks, yet the mass appeal of the Brontës can still draw greater audiences than most.

The Society has individual members scattered worldwide. But despite the importance of Brussels in the Brontë story, this is the first time a branch has been formed in that city. It is unusual in being a multinational group, as you might expect in the "capital of Europe". Outside Brussels you would be unlikely to find people of twenty or thirty different nationalities coming together at the meetings of a local branch. Members are from every European country and first read the Brontës' novels in their own language (not just the Brontës', of course, for all the great English novels have proved extraordinarily successful in reaching readers worldwide).

On the face of it Brussels may seem an incongruous setting for a literary venture centred around the highly romantic figures of the Brontë family – a city of committees and councils, representations and delegations, meetings and summits to which people come to do business, a city of bureaucrats. Our group does indeed include "bureaucrats". But of course they have their romantic side as much as anyone else. And of course Brussels is more than the city of European bureaucracy. It has its romantic side too.

Although it has never attracted a fraction of the literary tourists who throng to Haworth, ever since the publication of *Villette* in 1853 there has been a steady stream of literary pilgrims to the city that inspired it. When I was embarking on my Brontë venture in Brussels I read about those who had been here before me. The Brontës' stay in the city has always had a particular fascination for the relatively few readers who relish Charlotte's last novel. For these admirers of *Villette*, the site of the Brussels boarding school where Charlotte and Emily stayed in 1842-43 is as much a literary shrine as the Parsonage in Haworth, and a century after its demolition they still come to visit the site.

But although there has been no lack of interest in Charlotte's Brussels adventure over the years, few Brontë enthusiasts spend much time in Belgium's rather unloved capital. Like the delegates flying in for summits, tourists, even literary ones, rarely stay for more than a day or two. In the second half of the nineteenth century, at the height of *Villette*'s popularity

1

in America – where for a long time it was more appreciated than in Britain – some American fans would include Brussels on their European tour mainly to seek out Lucy Snowe's *Pensionnat*; this mission accomplished, they soon moved on to the greater attractions of the larger European capitals. Today, a coachload of Brontë Society members occasionally descends for a few days. But even scholars and biographers have tended to pay only fleeting visits to the city and, once here, the main feeling may be disappointment that the Pensionnat is no more.

And yet one of the most gratifying of my Brontë discoveries in Brussels was the extent of the interest I encountered among people living in the capital. My own interest brought me into contact with many latter-day enthusiasts, and this book is an account of how we came together, how a shared passion evolved into a literary association, how people become fascinated by writers' works and lives and the places where they have lived, and what forms this fascination can take.

Some of our members are Belgian, but many of us are foreign residents in the city, expatriates like Charlotte and Emily. Much of what is described in *Villette* and *The Professor* still resonates with us today and most of us can understand the French that peppers these novels without resorting to footnotes. Like Charlotte and Emily, some of us have studied French in this city. Like foreigners anywhere, we will have experienced some degree of what is today termed "culture shock" even if today's expatriates are rarely such acute sufferers as Charlotte Brontë!

Brussels itself has done little to commemorate the Brontë sisters' stay. Byron, who spent only a few days here, has been given a plaque, and there is one on the spot where Verlaine shot Rimbaud after a falling-out between the two on a brief visit to the city. A plaque has even been given to Baudelaire, of all people, who came here to escape from his creditors only to take such a violent dislike to Belgium that he started to write a book about how much he hated it. But although two of Charlotte Brontë's four novels are set in Brussels, there was no plaque for her until the Brontë Society itself put one up for her and Emily in 1979. Doubtless this is partly Charlotte's fault. If she had been less scathing in her remarks about the city's inhabitants, it might be more inclined to remember her today. But perhaps the city authorities could follow the example of the descendants of Monsieur and Madame Heger who cheerfully showed "pilgrims" around the Pensionnat, overcoming their irritation at Charlotte's fictional account and feeling some gratification at having harboured a now world-famous writer. Her prejudices about their country do not deter numerous Belgian readers from enjoying her work.

It may be that Brussels' silence is due to indifference as much as annoyance; the Brontës are English writers and the city is naturally more anxious to celebrate Belgian authors or those writing in the languages of Belgium. But the authorities are surely missing an opportunity to add to the city's appeal. There can be few tourists who have never heard of *Wuthering Heights* or *Jane Eyre*, but surprisingly few are aware that their authors lived for a time in the Belgian capital or that half Charlotte's mature novels were based on her time here.

Visitors passing through the city, then, will find little or no mention of the Brontës at the tourist office. But many foreigners who come to live here read *Villette*, having previously been unaware of Charlotte Brontë's Brussels sojourn, and then want to know whether the novel reflects her actual experiences. Newcomers to our group are often newcomers to Brussels itself, learning about Charlotte and Emily's time in the city while they themselves are adapting to life here. Charlotte's two-year stay in Brussels was overshadowed by negativity and grumpiness towards it while there and vindictiveness towards it in retrospect. Yet the power of *Villette* and of her life story makes her legacy today a positive one for many visitors and residents of the city whose inhabitants she reviled but by which she was haunted for the rest of her life.

In the words of one member, on joining the group shortly after arriving in the city: "I have been in Brussels for two months, and throughout that time *Villette* has been my wonderful companion." Through our group, many people have found real-life companions to accompany them on their discovery of Brussels and of the Brontë sisters' time here.

1. *Along Rue de la Loi*

When I moved to Brussels in 2004 to take up a post as a translator, I knew little about the city and pictured it as a place of bureaucracy rather than of charm or adventure. First impressions confirmed this. I found myself working in a huge building with interminable corridors, all exactly alike; on my second or third day I got out of the lift at the wrong floor, walked all the way to what I imagined was my office, went in and sat down at the computer before realising my mistake. That building was next to "Rond-Point Schuman". In any other city Robert Schumann is a romantic composer, but the Brussels roundabout refers to the Robert Schuman who was one of the founding fathers of the European Union.

So in those first few days I found Brussels as unromantic as I had anticipated. However, almost as soon as I emerged from my ministry-like building and began to explore the "European quarter", I had glimpses of a very different city even within that quarter. I would walk past the vast metal and glass Berlaymont building, the main seat of the European Commission, and in a minute or two find myself on the cobblestone pavement of a quiet street lined with tall narrow picturesque houses with gables, oriel windows and decorative brickwork. Or I would chance upon a gracious square from an era long pre-dating the European district, hidden away behind the office blocks housing the Commission's "directorates-general" along streets with names like Rue du Commerce and Rue de la Science.

One lunch hour, I decided to explore further and walked along the similarly unexcitingly named Rue de la Loi (Law Street) which connects the European district with the centre of the city, a long straight street lined with office buildings. A traffic thoroughfare, it is certainly not a good example of the charm to be found in the European quarter, being perhaps the most charmless thing in it.

Venturing further than on any of my previous excursions, I reached the end of the street, past the Belgian parliament building, and found myself by the city's central park, Parc de Bruxelles. I turned left alongside the park and realised that my twenty-minute walk from the heart of the European quarter had brought me to Rue Royale, which leads to Place Royale with its royal palace and art museums. As a newcomer to Brussels I was still often taken aback by the small scale of the city Thackeray condescendingly described as "Lilliputian" on a visit in the 1840s.* Although its population has swelled to a million since his time, Brussels still has a Lilliputian, provincial feel compared with Paris or London, but it does have its share of elegant classical buildings and streets, one of which I was now walking along. This was a different city to the one I had just left, a city of serene eighteenth-century architecture.

Just before Place Royale, on the side of Rue Royale opposite the park, I came to a statue of some city dignitary, behind which a flight of steps led down to a small street at right angles to Rue Royale and at a much lower level. Looking down – although I had not yet got my bearings in the city – I sensed that these steps were the transition to yet another Brussels. The tall spire in the distance, which I recognised as that of the town hall in Grand Place, told me that the steps led in the direction of the old centre. The plunge down to that lower city gave me a sense of adventure and romance, of something to explore.

Later, I was to realise that I had been standing on the edge of the "Upper Town" built in the eighteenth and nineteenth centuries, looking down at the "Lower", medieval town. But it would be some time before I would realise the significance of those steps down to the quiet street below and of the site where it is located.

I was soon in Place Royale – tranquil despite the rumbling trams and groups of tourists wandering from museum to museum – and here, parallel to the flight of steps I had just passed, was another drop to an even lower level opening up a vista of the old city below. This was the much more spectacular descent of "Mont des Arts", terraced gardens leading down from the museum area to Central Station and Grand Place.

It was time to return to work, so I hurried back to my office at Rond-Point Schuman. I took the metro rather than walking back along Rue de la Loi. I didn't know then how important my exploration along that unappealing street was to prove for my life in Brussels.

I did feel, however, that my lunchtime excursion had taken me into another world, or rather two other worlds: the gracious and elegant city of Rue Royale and Place Royale, and that sense of another, older and more secret town down the plunging steps beyond the statue, that odd sensation of adventure and romance that had come to me as I looked down and that I couldn't quite explain.

2. *Reading Villette in Brussels*

A few months later I did something I was to find many people do after moving to Brussels. I read – in my case re-read – Charlotte Brontë's *Villette*.

I barely remembered the novel from my first reading, when it had made a confusing and unpleasant impression on me. Unlike the intoxicating experience of reading *Jane Eyre* at the age of twelve or thirteen, *Villette* left a sour taste in the mouth. Far from lifting me to heights of passion, it drew me down into the morose and claustrophobic "shadow world" of cold Lucy Snowe.

This time was different. Lucy Snowe's world was now as vivid and intense for me, in its way, as Jane's had been. Partly because I was so much older and must have been too young to enter her dark world at the first reading. But another reason was that like Lucy Snowe I was a foreigner abroad – in the very city in which Lucy is lonely and homesick, as well as in the grip of unrequited love.

I was none of these things myself and was growing to like Brussels, but Lucy's loneliness and homesickness as a teacher at Mme Beck's Pensionnat de Demoiselles took me back to another less happy time in another place - the small town in northern France where I had spent a year as a teaching assistant during my French degree course. Although, unlike Mme Beck's establishment, it was not a boarding school, the German assistant and I were accommodated in an apartment in one of the school buildings. After school hours, the only people inhabiting the place were the caretaker and his family, the other assistant and myself. If I had exerted myself, no doubt I could have made more friends in the town and spent a happier year abroad. But like Lucy Snowe and her creator, I had solitary hours. I was homesick and, like Charlotte/Lucy, didn't always find my companions congenial. And I did not take to teaching any more than Charlotte (Lucy's taming of her unruly pupils, as when she locks one of them in a classroom cupboard, must have been pure wish fulfilment on Charlotte's part). When the weekend arrived, despite invitations to the homes of friendly colleagues – kind invitations that my shyness made me dread as much as Charlotte and Emily Brontë dreaded Sunday lunch with the British chaplain Mr Jenkins and his family – I sometimes found myself alone in the school with its deserted classrooms and garden, as solitary as Lucy in the empty Pensionnat during the long vacation.

Like Charlotte and Lucy, I felt there was a barrier between myself and those around me. I had spent years studying French, yet I seemed to be in alien territory. A not uncommon expatriate perception, but like Charlotte/Lucy I was all too prone to sense a barrier that was in fact the result of my own reserve.

During this time I read a lot of French literature, immersing myself in it as Charlotte did, though without a fiery Monsieur Heger to guide me. I experienced France more through its literature than through my unsatisfactory everyday life. But despite feelings of isolation, even in the school routine I, like Charlotte, did experience some aspects of the foreign culture so intensely that I never forgot them. I would always remember the simple but delicious dishes that introduced me to the delights of everyday French fare in the drab setting of the school canteen. Like Charlotte I would spend part of my modest wages on little treats in *boulangeries*. Like her I also savoured with pleasure the foreign language around me. Jane Eyre relishes her ability to speak French with Adèle. Charlotte Brontë seized greedily on an opportunity to practise the language of M. Heger with a Frenchman she met on a train in England.

But reading *Villette* took me back not only to that homesick time in France but also to a still earlier time in my life. It brought a renewal of the intensity with which I had first read the Brontës' books when I was not much older than the young Jane Eyre.

Over the years I had read books by and about the Brontës, but now I felt a revival of interest in them, particularly in Charlotte. I wanted to know more about the experiences that had led her to write her Brussels novels. Previously I had always visualised her in the Parsonage and on the moors – as described in Mrs Gaskell's *Life of Charlotte Brontë*, since I had never been there myself. Now, because Brussels had become a real place to me, I wondered for the first time about Charlotte's years there.

I read *The Professor*, finding even this unpolished first novel full of interest when read in Brussels because of its evocation of the streets where Crimsworth walks in search of Frances, the Protestant cemetery where he finds her, the little lodging in which he visits her. I read modern biographies and learned more about the Pensionnat Heger in Rue d'Isabelle, the school where Charlotte and Emily lived and studied, and wondered if anything remained of the Quartier Isabelle. *Villette* contained evocative descriptions not just of the school and its garden but of the streets among which they stood, lying somewhat forgotten and overlooked far below the busy Rue Royale. I knew from the biographies that the area had changed greatly since then but was not sure whether anything was still standing from the Brontës' time.

Some time passed before I had time to investigate. Other things took precedence. I was too occupied with house-hunting to hunt for the Pensionnat.

But one day I went back to Rue Royale. Walking along the stretch that goes past the Park, I noticed the statue by which I had paused on my lunchtime exploration some months earlier. This time I looked at the name on the plinth and saw that the statesman was a General Belliard. I did not know who he was but the name and the steps leading down behind him to the street below now rang a bell. I remembered reading that the "Belliard steps" led down to the Pensionnat. I descended them, only to find myself not in Rue d'Isabelle but in a street called Baron Horta, with nothing to indicate that this was the site of the school. To the right was the headquarters of the Fortis bank, to the left another twentieth-century building, the Palais des Beaux-Arts arts centre (known as "Bozar"), designed in the 1920s by the Art Nouveau architect Victor Horta, after whom the street is named. Bozar is an important place in Brussels, as it houses the city's biggest concert hall. Ahead of me was the entry to an uninspiring shopping centre called Galerie Ravenstein. At this low level, the graceful spire of the Town Hall in Grand Place, visible from the top of the steps, was out of sight. I could see no plaque or other commemoration of the Pensionnat Heger or of the Brontës.

I felt disappointed. There seemed to be nothing at all left of the area the Brontës had known.

I lost interest in the site of the Pensionnat until I happened to read the introduction to *Villette* by Helen Cooper, the editor of my 2004 Penguin edition, in which she writes:

> In June 2001 I visited Brussels, where, although people knew of Charlotte Brontë and of her novel *Jane Eyre*, no one I met knew that Brontë had lived and studied in the city or written *Villette*, a title that was her fictional name for Brussels. No one knew the whereabouts of the Rue Isabelle, the street historically associated with the Pensionnat Heger where Charlotte and her sister Emily had studied in 1842 and where Charlotte returned as a teacher in 1843-4 hoping for enough education and experience to set up a school in her home town of Haworth in Yorkshire.

Like so many Brontë scholars, Helen Cooper paid only a flying visit to Brussels, the city where Charlotte spent almost two of the thirty-nine years of her life. Her mission for the day she was there was to visit the site of the Pensionnat (where "lie the shadows of Brontë, Heger, Lucy Snowe, Madame Beck and Monsieur Paul, haunting Brussels through all its changes"), the Cathedral where Charlotte/Lucy confessed and the park in which Lucy wanders one night during a Belgian national *fête*. The last two were easy but she found trying to locate the site of the Pensionnat and Rue d'Isabelle a frustrating task:

> ... when I reached the statue from which one is supposed to be able to look down four flights of stairs to the Rue Isabelle I looked down and saw only a small shopping centre.

She concluded her account of her pilgrimage to Brussels by saying:

> I would have had a much easier but far less adventurous time if I had had access to Eric Ruijssenaars' book *Charlotte Brontë's Promised Land: the Pensionnat Heger and other Brontë Places in Brussels*.

At last help was in sight! I found out that this book, written in English by a Dutch researcher, had been published in 2000 by the Brontë Society and could be ordered from the Brontë Parsonage Museum bookshop in Haworth.

I had never been to Haworth. I had imagined the Parsonage and the village for so long I had always feared that seeing the real place would be a disappointment. The Pensionnat, conversely, no longer existed and I was eager to find out as much about it as possible in order to reconstruct it in my imagination in the streets of Brussels.

Statue of General Belliard at the top of the Belliard steps
(*Dexia Bank postcard collection, 1904*)

3. *Down the Belliard Steps*

Eric Ruijssenaars' book, *Charlotte Brontë's Promised Land* (there is also a sequel, *The Pensionnat Revisited*) proved to be the key that I, like Helen Cooper before me, needed in order to unlock the door to the Pensionnat and finally succeed in seeing the enchanted world of *Villette*, in imagination, in the streets of Brussels today. Eric's book recreates the lost world of the little bit of Brussels that Charlotte herself recreated in *Villette* and *The Professor*. Even in her time, the Pensionnat – with its large casement windows opening onto its garden, a magical garden hidden away behind its walls amid peaceful streets – was a secret world lying below the bustling thoroughfare of Rue Royale.

Since the construction of Rue Royale in the 1770s, Rue d'Isabelle, in its day an important street, had sunk into obscurity. It was built in the seventeenth century by the Infanta Isabella, daughter of Philip II of Spain and Governor of the Low Countries, as a royal route linking the Palace with the Cathedral. Once a new route for that purpose had been provided by Rue Royale, Rue d'Isabelle became a tranquil backwater. Even in Charlotte's day, visitors to the city would stumble on it only by chance, descending the steep steps from the busy Upper Town created in the eighteenth century to the low-lying, older and very different world of the Isabelle quarter on the cusp of the oldest part of town, around Grand Place.

Charlotte herself must have been very aware of the Pensionnat's position between the *Haute-Ville* or Upper Town of the aristocracy, with its broad, well-lit streets and rattling carriages, and the older, darker, grimmer *Basse-Ville*, unfamiliar and fascinating to her with its picturesque old houses and narrow streets, which Lucy explores in off-duty hours. On her visit down in the old town to the house of the sinister Mme Walravens, grandmother of the long-dead fiancée of M. Paul, where she learns many of the secrets of his life, Lucy describes the deserted square where the old woman lives, grass growing between the flags, a storm threatening in the dark sky overhead. The description can still seem apt today when walking in the old streets of Brussels or crossing one of its quiet squares under a lowering sky. Many of the buildings today date from after Charlotte's time. But much of Brussels is still a city of narrow streets, made slightly claustrophobic by tall terraced houses, and empty squares with grass between the paving stones. Whole swathes of it are eerily silent and abandoned for a capital city. A city not without charm, but a charm that is often somewhat melancholy.

Not long after reading Eric's book I was to meet him and learn that he was a fan of Lewis Carroll. He drew a fanciful parallel between Charlotte's descent into the strange foreign world at the bottom of the Belliard steps – a Continental, Catholic world where everything seemed topsy-turvy and

Rue d'Isabelle: the little houses built by Isabella for the crossbowmen
(*Brussels City Archives*)

perplexing to her northern, Protestant mind – and Alice's descent down the rabbit hole into Wonderland.

Sepia photos in his book showed Rue d'Isabelle as it was in the mid-nineteenth century, a sleepy charming street lined with little houses built to compensate the members of the archers' guild whose land was expropriated by Isabella in order to build her street.

The first thing you see when you open Eric's book is an 1843 street map of the Isabelle quarter set alongside a map of the area as it is today. The entire quarter was demolished at the turn of the twentieth century when a rail link was built between the North and South Stations, a project that included the construction of Central Station not far from the Pensionnat site. Like so much of old Brussels, the area was also a victim of Leopold II's vision of Brussels as a modern city of wide boulevards. The realisation of this vision created some elegant boulevards but also started the trend of insensitive development that has marred so much of the city.

The transformation wrought by Leopold's urban architects has always made things difficult for visitors seeking the site of the Pensionnat. Many have been as frustrated as I was initially in the search for some indication of where the school used to stand, some remaining clue to the lost Quartier Isabelle in today's street layout.

From Eric's book I learned that in 1979 the Brontë Society had placed a plaque to mark the site of the Pensionnat. However, it is so difficult to spot that I later realised I had twice walked past it without noticing it.

But one day – Eric's book, with its "then and now" street plans, in my hand – I descended the Belliard steps again and finally established where the places I had visualised in imagination had actually stood. When you reached the bottom of the steps in Charlotte's time – different steps then, steeper and narrower, and many more of them since the Isabelle quarter was at a lower level than today's street – you crossed the narrow Rue d'Isabelle to the door of the Pensionnat straight opposite you with its sign *Pensionnat de Demoiselles Heger-Parent*. "Parent" was the maiden name of Mme Heger, who was already director of the school before her marriage. Rue d'Isabelle lay parallel to the street at the top of the steps, Rue Royale, whereas today's Rue Baron Horta is at right angles to it, running in the same direction as the steps.

Once again I found myself in this unremarkable-looking street. From the plans, I established that most of the classrooms had been located where the bank building to the right stands today, while the garden and the entrance

Rue d'Isabelle, c. 1900 (*Brussels City Archives*)

to the school had been on the site of "Bozar" (the Palais des Beaux-Arts), the arts centre on the left.

This time, looking up, I spotted the Brontë Society plaque to the left of the entrance to "Bozar", placed so high it's no wonder passers-by rarely notice it. Even the most persevering Brontë tourists have been known to walk straight past it.

Having at last succeeded in pinpointing the site of the Pensionnat, I did feel disappointed that so little is left of the bit of Brussels associated with

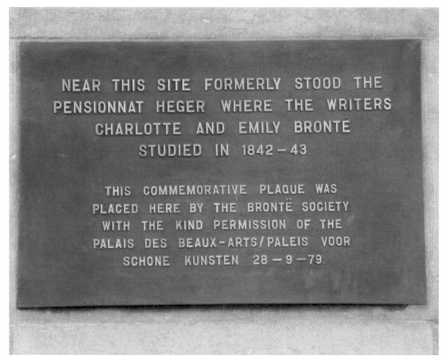

Brontë Society plaque on Palais des Beaux-Arts ("Bozar")

Bozar (the plaque is above the tiny window to the left of the awning with "BOZAR" on it)

the Brontës; it was not until later that I was to discover that traces of the old quarter do in fact remain, offering tantalising glimpses of what has been lost. Admittedly, the difficulty of finding any traces of the sisters' sojourn heightens the satisfaction when you do come across clues. The fact that the world of the Pensionnat is today a lost world adds to its allure.

On the moors around Haworth there are signposts in Japanese for Brontë tourists. No such help is provided in Brussels, but as Helen Cooper points out in her introduction to *Villette*, this indifference does have the effect of turning a literary pilgrimage to the city into an adventure.

Over the next few years, the Quartier Isabelle, demolished a century ago, was to become the most real and alive part of the city for me, a starting point and gateway for my acquaintance with it.

It lives, of course, in the pages on *Villette*. Thanks to the intensity and minuteness of Charlotte's descriptions, anyone who reads the novel can visualise the Pensionnat without ever visiting Brussels. But now that I knew about the real place and had stood on the site of the school, it gripped my imagination in a new way. There was something incongruous and surreal in the thought that Charlotte and Emily had been on this spot so far from Haworth Moor. Once they had left the Pensionnat behind and returned to the Parsonage their time there must have seemed like a dream. For Emily, Brussels was doubtless no more than an irrelevant interlude. Apart from acquiring some learning there – some music and foreign literature that may have helped to nourish *Wuthering Heights*, perhaps even then starting to grow in her imagination – the months at the Pensionnat seem to have left no imprint on her, and we have no words of hers to tell us what they meant to her.

But for Charlotte her time there was highly significant, a dream come true that gradually turned into a nightmare. When she first conceived the idea of studying in Belgium – born of the urge to spread her wings, the need to qualify herself to start her own school if she was to escape the slavery of being a governess, and her friend Mary Taylor's glowing reports of the city's sights – Charlotte called Brussels her "promised land". She reached it through sheer determination and for the first half of her stay the promised land seems to have lived up to her expectations. She was much happier in the role of pupil than as a teacher and particularly happy to be the pupil of M. Heger. In her second year, of course, when she returned without Emily, it all went sour. She was soon bewailing the isolation of her life at the school and the uncongeniality of its inhabitants, M. Heger excepted, and indeed of all Belgians. The man she was falling in love with formed part of a happy family from which she was naturally excluded, for she had not thought it appropriate to take up the Hegers' kind invitation to join their family circle in the evenings. She sank into depression as she had done not only during every previous foray away from the Parsonage but all too often in the Parsonage itself. Wherever Charlotte was – Parsonage, Pensionnat, governess in a country house – life always seemed to her to be happening elsewhere. This was indeed the case at the Pensionnat in the summer vacation. With nowhere to go when everyone else departed on holiday, she was left pacing the empty classrooms, where her state of mind became so morbid she was driven one day to go to confession at the Cathedral to relieve her loneliness. In Brussels, as everywhere else, Charlotte Brontë all too soon ended up feeling dissatisfied and isolated.

Yet her inner life there was so intense that ten years after leaving the city she was to relive her stay there in the darkly vivid world of *Villette*.

Mrs Gaskell sketches dramatically the background to the real place in which Charlotte lived out her inner drama; Eric completes Gaskell's account and corrects some inaccuracies. Thanks to them I learned about the area not only as it was in Charlotte's time but also in earlier periods. Charlotte too must have heard something of its history. The old legends hinted at in *Villette*, with its story of a nun buried alive under the garden as a punishment for some crime, were partly invented but doubtless also based on facts and local lore gleaned during her stay there.

The name she gives to Rue d'Isabelle in *Villette*, Rue Fossette, must have been inspired by "Fossé-aux-Chiens" (dogs' ditch or channel), the old name for the area later occupied by the Pensionnat garden. It is thought to refer both to the kennels which housed the hunting dogs of the Dukes of Brabant, whose palace stood on the site of today's royal palace, and to one of the channels for the streams that ran downhill from the park to the river Senne. Like so much of Brussels – as shown by the *étangs* (ponds) mentioned by Charlotte and still to be found all over the city in unexpected places – the Isabelle area stood on marshy, swampy land which had to be drained. She would have heard, too, that Rue d'Isabelle followed the line of the old city wall, though by the 1840s little remained visible of the ramparts or towers. The statue of General Belliard was there in her time but the steps leading down from it to Rue d'Isabelle were not then known as the Belliard steps. They were the "Escalier de la Bibliothèque", named after a mansion that stood on the site of the staircase before it was constructed. The house was built by Isabelle for the Master of the Archers' Guild and in its latter days used to store books rescued from the old ducal palace nearby when it burned down in the mid-eighteenth century. Charlotte would also have heard that there had been a medieval hospice on the site of the Pensionnat garden and that the same site was later used as an exercise ground by the city's crossbowmen.

Thanks to my reading I could now picture not only the lost world of the Pensionnat and its garden but also the various layers of the site's previous history – the old hospice, the practice ground for the crossbowmen who defended the city from attack, the secret underground passage through which they could take flight if besieged, and which is thought to have inspired Charlotte's tale of the buried nun. All this had fed into the

Panoramic view of Rue d'Isabelle and the Pensionnat
(*Brussels City Archives*)

wonderfully Gothic atmosphere of Charlotte's novel, what the British critic Gerald Cumberland, who visited the Pensionnat just before it was demolished, called "the spirit of romance and mystery that suffuses each page of *Villette*." *

4. *Pilgrims to the Pensionnat*

Gerald Cumberland was one of the many people who visited the Pensionnat before its demolition in 1910, or who tried to locate its site once it had gone. In Eric's book, I read about some of these Brontë pilgrims before me who had happened upon the world of *Villette* at the bottom of the Belliard steps.

While the Pensionnat still stood, literary pilgrims from America, where *Villette* enjoyed a popularity it never knew in Britain, would take in the city as part of their European tour and set out from their hotel with a copy of *Villette* or *The Professor* under their arm to seek Madame Beck's Pensionnat de Demoiselles. There was always an element of challenge in the quest. *Villette* had to be consulted for topographical references, clues followed up, directions sought from local shopkeepers. But after a few wrong turnings, these hopeful tourists usually succeeded in locating General Belliard's statue and found themselves descending the steps behind him. Once at the door they were seeking, many were brave enough to ring the bell. What is surprising is that members of the Heger family, despite all they had suffered from Charlotte Brontë's acid pen, seemed happy enough to show their unannounced visitors round the classrooms and listen to them rhapsodising about the author of *Villette*.

I read about how a group of *Villette*-mad American girls, in defiance of their parents' scepticism, set off from their Brussels hotel in search of the Pensionnat. It was a sunny summer's day, but for them "*Villette* was more real than that June day". In fact their quest turned out to be remarkably easy. Their hotel was in Rue Royale, by the park, and they soon spotted the Belliard statue and the steps they recognised from the description in the novel.

> We descended into the narrow, noiseless street and stood – an awe-struck group – before the great square house, upon the door-plate of which we read 'Pensionnat de Demoiselles. Heger-Parent'.

The door was opened by a teacher at the school who turned out to have been a pupil there at the same time as Charlotte Brontë. Although her comments betrayed scant admiration for Charlotte or her books, she gave the excited girls a guided tour, leading them through the classroom where Charlotte and Emily used to sit in a corner in the back row and into the garden with its Allée Défendue, the path that was out of bounds to the demoiselles because the boys' school, the Athenée, was on the other side of the garden wall. She even let them pick leaves from the pear trees as souvenirs, which they showed to their parents back at the hotel as proof that their adventure had really taken place.

Thus, as early as the 1860s, when Adeline Trafton – from whose travel memoirs this account is taken* – visited the Pensionnat with her friends, the Brontë sisters' stay there had taken on a mythical character. Entering the school had all the excitement of stumbling on something you have imagined to exist only in the pages of a favourite novel and then miraculously find in real life. The door at the bottom of the steps was like those doors that lead the heroes or heroines of fairy stories into another world, a dimension outside the everyday one. Except that for Adeline and other literary tourists in the second half of the nineteenth century, this door actually led into what was still recognisably Lucy Snowe's school. To the four girls and others like them, who returned to their lives in America bearing their pear-tree leaves, the experience at the bottom of the Belliard steps must have seemed truly dream-like.

I also read haunting accounts by the last pilgrims to see the Pensionnat before it was demolished. It was one of the last buildings in the quartier to be flattened and the Heger family had ceased to have any connection with it, yet none of these Brontë enthusiasts had any difficulty in recognising it as Mme Beck's establishment. Gerald Cumberland had to bribe the caretaker to let him into the doomed building, by now deserted. Wandering alone in the Allée Défendue as twilight descended, he had an even more powerful sense of communion with the spirits of Charlotte and Emily Brontë than he had felt on the moors of Haworth.* Just months later the school had gone the way of the rest of the quarter.

What was the fascination of the Pensionnat for these literary pilgrims? First and foremost, of course, it attracted them because it is depicted so vividly in *Villette* – more vividly than any other place in Charlotte's novels; we don't feel we know Thornfield Hall nearly as intimately as we do the school in Brussels. Then there was the thrill of feeling themselves members of a select band; *Villette's* following has always been tiny compared with that of *Jane Eyre* and *Wuthering Heights*. There was the excitement of playing detective, so far from the usual track beaten by Brontë pilgrims to the door of the Parsonage. There was the incongruity of Charlotte and Emily's Brussels adventure; it was intriguing to imagine Emily, in particular, in an urban and foreign setting so far from her Yorkshire moors. And the added incongruity that the scene of Charlotte Brontë's undeclared, unrequited love was not those moors, perceived since *Wuthering Heights* as the appropriate background for hopeless passion, but what she calls "unromantic, unpoetic" Belgium* and the cloistered atmosphere of a girls' boarding school.

These enthusiasts of Charlotte's Brussels period were aware of its importance for her life and novels. Brussels was the place where she first really fell in love with someone encountered in real life. It was a hopeless love which drove her back upon her writing for solace and wish-fulfilment. Writing had always provided an escape from frustration, but the novels she wrote after Brussels had a new power and realism; it is likely that her

The Pensionnat and its garden
(*Brontë Parsonage Museum*)

painful experience with Heger was at least partly responsible for this new maturity.

Of course he enhanced her talent in less painful ways too. Although he was training her to be a teacher rather than encouraging her to become a professional writer, he took her writing seriously and made her think more critically about style and structure. Unresponsive as Heger the (married) man was – had to be – to her appeals for his affection, Heger the teacher's response to her work, while drawing attention to its faults, gave her a discipline and confidence which helped to make *Jane Eyre*, written less than three years after leaving Brussels, the beautifully crafted novel it is. As a man he became a model not just for M. Paul but also for Mr Rochester. But the notes he made in the margins of her French essays were etched in her mind as indelibly as his personality in her emotions.

After the publication of Charlotte Brontë's letters to Heger in 1913, enthusiasts of her Brussels period had added reason to see the period as a turning point for her. Marion Spielmann claims that "Charlotte Brontë....was greatly in her art, and to some degree in her emotion, the product of the Rue d'Isabelle"* and Frederika Macdonald that "[She left] her broken heart buried in that silent, secret place" and then revisited the grave of her love in her novels.*

5. *Eric*

After reading a book that interests me I always want to learn more about the author; I couldn't have read the Brontës' novels without wishing to know all about the people who wrote them. Having read Eric's book I started to wonder who Eric Ruijssenaars was and what had prompted him to do this research.

The origin of his interest was hinted at in the acknowledgements in his book, in a reference to a friend who had inspired his interest in the Brontës and to impress whom he had written it. Apart from that, all I knew about him was that he was Dutch. This meant that he was a native speaker of one of the two languages of Brussels, which gave him something of an insider's view of the subject. But as a Dutchman in Belgium, he was also an outsider trying to make sense of a complex bit of Brussels local history, a task made more challenging by the errors that have crept into accounts of the Quartier Isabelle and the history of the school from Mrs Gaskell onwards. Eric's book reads in places like a detective story as he chases up clues and sifts conflicting records. You sense that he had become totally absorbed in the many-layered history of the Quartier. A scholar from a country that was flat, prosaic and well ordered, he had wandered down the Belliard steps into a world at a different level from the everyday one, touched with the mystery and romance of *Villette*.

One reason for seeking Eric's acquaintance was that I had conceived the idea of forming a branch of the Brontë Society in Brussels. Thanks to his books I now knew that I was only one in a long line of visitors to the city whose imagination had been stirred by Charlotte and Emily's stay. Most of them had come for only a day or two. But I was a resident in the city with time to pursue this interest, and there must be other people living here who shared my fascination. I wanted to make contact with them but wasn't yet sure how. Eric Ruijssenaars did not live in Brussels, yet he was to be the first link in the human chain I was to forge.

Thanks to the Internet it proved easy to contact him and we were soon exchanging e-mails about my idea of starting up a Brontë group in Brussels. Eric made his living as an archivist, often doing genealogical research for Americans descended from Dutch settlers in the United States. He lived in the old university town of Leiden and since one of his literary idols was Lewis Carroll I imagined Leiden to be the Dutch equivalent of Oxford and Eric as a donnish figure cycling around its medieval buildings and dreaming his days away in libraries. What was certain was that he was an Anglophile, an avid follower of cricket and reader of Dickens, Dr Johnson and Pepys as well as Carroll, though not all his tastes were for the antique since he also appreciated *EastEnders*. A keen gardener, after weeding his vegetable beds he would sit on a bench reading his English books,

Eric

surrounded by the fruits of his labours. His e-mails sometimes contained bulletins on both activities: "Potatoes doing well", "David has now married Dora".

When we later met he proved to have some of the kind of eccentricities I had imagined, such as the notes he made in minuscule handwriting on tiny pieces of paper with which the young Brontës would have felt at home.

In the course of our correspondence he told me something about his first encounter with the Brontës through the Dutch friend acknowledged in his book, Elisabeth – "Elle" to her friends – who introduced him both to *Villette*, her favourite novel, and to Brussels. As his interest grew he started reading all he could on Brontë connections in the city. One day he wrote to the city archives to ask if they had a plan of the Pensionnat. They were able to provide one dating from not long after the Brontës' time, and it was once he had seen this plan that his research really took off.

It was another woman who gave him the idea of turning his research into a book. In 1993 he went to Brussels to meet a coachload of Brontë Society members who were visiting the city to celebrate the Society's centenary. The excursion was led by the journalist and novelist Charlotte Cory, who guided her troupe, dressed in Victorian costume, to take tea at the Ambassador's Residence on the anniversary of Charlotte Brontë's birth and to picnic on *brioches* and *pistolets* by the bandstand in the park where Lucy Snowe wanders on the night of the fête.

Cory's enthusiasm for the Brontës often had more than a dash of the eccentric and flamboyant, as when she held a competition in Haworth to find look-alikes of Emily's dog Keeper. It was an enthusiasm that was not always uncritical, and she chose Charlotte Brontë as her "villain" in the Independent Magazine's "Heroes and Villains" column*, on the grounds that Charlotte was over-interested in her male employers, demonised her female ones and used her novels to work off grudges. She had always been intrigued by Brontë connections in Brussels and suggested to Eric that he apply for a scholarship from the Brontë Society to pursue his Brussels research. His book was written thanks to the grant he was awarded.

Eric grew up in the Dutch province of North Brabant, on the border with Belgium, which in the old days, before the division of the Low Countries, formed part of the Duchy of Brabant, an area that also included the modern-day province of Flemish Brabant and Brussels (today a separate region within Flemish Brabant). Eric liked to attribute his special feeling for Brussels to the fact that in the Middle Ages it was the capital of the Duchy. He loved the city from the first time he set foot there in search of Charlotte Brontë's "Promised Land".

6. *Selina*

One of the attractions of Eric's books were the bold black and white illustrations showing the Quartier Isabelle in the Brontës' time. They are panoramic views of the Pensionnat and its garden set amid encircling streets. Each cobble of Rue d'Isabelle, each roof-tile of the little houses lining it and each tree along the *Allée Défendue* is clearly and lovingly worked in pen and ink.

In the course of our correspondence Eric told me that the artist, his friend Selina Busch, had once tried unsuccessfully to form a branch of the Brontë Society in the Netherlands. I wrote to Selina to suggest forming a branch made up of members living in both the Low Countries and was soon corresponding with her as well as with Eric. As we exchanged e-mails I began to build up an impression of my second Dutch correspondent as I had of my first.

An individualist just as much as Eric, Selina had studied design and architecture, trained as a bookbinder and was now doing book restoration work in the archives of her town.

Even more than Eric, who was similarly absorbed in the past to which his studies related, Selina lived in the world of her mind. Facebook and mobile phones were not for her any more than for him. Her universe had been shaped by the literature and art of the past; her fascination with the Brontës extended to the Victorian period in general. I later visited her in her exquisite little house. Apart from a few concessions to the twenty-first century, such as the television from which she soaked up British costume dramas, it was a nineteenth-century bubble, furnished with antiques, the walls crowded with posters of paintings by Millais and Waterhouse.

Over the next few years I was to meet many people, from many different countries, whose fascination with the past and its literature found a focus in nineteenth-century literature and particularly in the Brontës. As we sat in her little Victorian house, Selina told me about how she came to enter that world.

7. *An unbroken thread*

Despite her dissatisfaction with many aspects of the late twentieth and early twenty-first century world that it was her lot to inhabit physically, Selina's first encounter with the Brontës, typically for someone of her generation, had been not through a book but through a film, a television adaptation. The 1983 BBC series of *Jane Eyre* starring Zelah Clarke and Timothy Dalton was broadcast on Dutch television on Sunday evenings when she was a young teenager.

Like most people of thirteen she was insecure, searching for an identity. From the first episode she felt a sense of recognition and identification, those words so often used by people attempting to describe a book that has made an impact in their youth.

In each successive week between episodes she became increasingly restless, living in the world of the novel and impatient for the following Sunday. But there was a problem. Hers was a religious household and she had no choice but to go to church. Since she didn't want to forgo a lie-in on Sunday mornings, she had to attend the evening service, which ended shortly before the start of the programme. She always cycled to church and there was a hill to climb on the way home. During the service her most fervent prayer was that it would be a short one so that she could grab her bike and pedal uphill fast enough to catch the opening credits and the music.

The series "transported me into a completely other place". Soon afterwards she borrowed the novel from the local library. Some words spoken by Jane to Rochester summed up its effect on her: "It is my spirit that addresses your spirit". The Brontës' spirit had touched her. Perhaps most teenagers experience something similar in those formative years.

It was the start of a journey of discovery. Jane Eyre, she found, had a creator and her name was Charlotte Brontë. With a basic knowledge of English she devoured Mrs Gaskell's *Life*, also from the local library, through which she discovered Charlotte's family and a distant place in England called Haworth.

Until then, reading had never come naturally to her. Hers was a visual fantasy world made up of pictures, drawing, making things. *Jane Eyre* was the first novel that really engaged her, but at first it drew her into a predominantly visual world. The Brontës were like a richly-coloured pattern which proved to be part of the great tapestry of the nineteenth-century world into which Selina escaped from the modern-day Dutch life from which she felt disconnected. When she picked up Dickens' novels she seemed to be walking in that world, penetrating all its layers, from the external and physical (Victorian houses, household objects, the clothes people wore) to the psychological and sociological aspects she came to

26

Selina

discover later on, the dark underside of Victorian society, the social unrest caused by industrialisation. Her friends and family said that she had been born in the wrong century. "As a teenager I was a drug addict. My drug was nineteenth-century England."

"Would you have liked to have been born in the nineteenth century?" I asked.

"Actually, no, I've come to realise I probably wouldn't choose to have been alive then. I prefer to live in it in imagination."

Her fascination inspired her creatively. She had found the perfect subject. Now, when she made things – a picture, a costume – they were a way of getting close to the Brontës' country and period.

It wasn't until she was out of her teens that she met Elle and Eric and other people who shared this feeling of affinity with the Brontës and their world. Typically, she summed up what the Brontës had meant to her with a visual and tactile image involving fabrics and colour and texture. "It's as if they are a brightly-coloured thread woven into my life that will never be broken, through which I have met people I feel connected with."

8. *Elle's story*

Selina's passion for the Brontës, ignited by reading *Jane Eyre* at the age of thirteen, took a new turn when she met Eric and Elle – a direction that was to lead her into this story.

Elle was good at transmitting her enthusiasm for *Villette* and Charlotte Brontë's Brussels to her friends.

For years I wondered about the, to me, mysterious "Elle". To me her name always evoked its French meaning. She was simply "She", someone I heard of through Eric and Selina. It was some time before I met her but I gradually came to realise that she was important in my story as well as theirs. Without her, Eric's book wouldn't have been written and Selina wouldn't have created the drawings that brought the Pensionnat to life for me. Had I not come across their work I might never have formed the Brussels group.

When I did at last meet her I saw an attractive woman who spoke ardently of the things that interested her, someone to whom superficial conventions meant little and who had an air of self-sufficiency, the aura of a person living in the world of her imagination, somewhat detached from the one around her.

Although our meeting was brief she later wrote about the path that led her to the Haworth moors and also to the Brussels of *Villette*. Like other people in this story who stumbled across books unaided and were changed by them, her background was anything but bookish. She grew up as a miner's daughter in the town of Brunssum not far from the border with Belgium. This Dutch place name sounds most unpoetic, and Brunssum is in fact a drab mining town.

Later, as a young woman now living in a university town – though she didn't study at university – she started borrowing books about nineteenth-century England. The first book she read about the Brontës, a biography of the family by the Dutch writer Johan van der Woude, *Het mysterie van de Brontës* (*The Mystery of the Brontës*) was soon followed by others. A black and white photograph of Main Street in Haworth with its cobbles and the slate roofs of the houses wet and shining after rain gripped her imagination as nothing had before. And when she read her first Brontë novel, which was *Villette* simply because it was the first one she came across, at a bookstall in a street market, she found in Lucy's emotional turmoil a reflection of her own emotions at that period in her life. When she finally came to read a biography of Charlotte Brontë she felt a sense of recognition and identification similar to that described by Selina.

She knew no-one who shared her interest in the Brontës, and this isolation intensified it all the more.

Elle

On her first trip to Haworth she arrived in the village by bus. As she approached, the heavens opened and her first sight of Main Street was of its cobblestones glistening in the rain, as in the photo that had so long formed part of her inner world, and her first glimpse of the moors was on a day of Brontëan storm and wind. She had a sense of homecoming when she saw those moors. They transported her back to Sundays in her childhood when her mother, who had grown up in the countryside, would take her and her

29

brothers and sister to walk in the heathland near their mining home town.

Apart from Haworth, the place whose Brontë associations most attracted her was Brussels – not far away across the Belgian border – where Charlotte experienced the most passionate and turbulent emotion of her life.

Her love for the Brontës continued to be a solitary one until, years later, she first found someone to share it, but only because she herself infected him with her own enthusiasm. On a trip to England organised for book-lovers, she met Eric Ruijssenaars, with whom she fell into conversation in a Hay-on-Wye bookshop. He had soon read *Villette* and accompanied her to Brussels, where the idea of his future research first began to germinate.

Not long after this she met Selina, through the Brontë Society. They had come to the Brontës by similar paths. Neither of them had grown up in the kind of household whose bookcases are lined with classic novels, or had studied literature in an academic way, but their first glimpse of the world of nineteenth-century England in the pages of a book had produced an instant feeling of affinity and belonging.

Their stories brought home to me the unique power of English nineteenth-century literature to draw people into its world. It is far enough removed from us to give us a sense of many things now lost, yet not too far to seem remote. It provides us with the romance we often feel is lacking in our own, yet its characters feel close to us.

It is often through its nineteenth-century literature that people from other cultures fall in love with the idea of England. For Elle, long before she first went there, it was a country of beautiful landscapes and timeless love stories, of Jane and Rochester, Elizabeth Bennet and Mr Darcy. She would become one of the countless tourists who, when they visit our country, see us not as we are today but through the medium of Jane Austen and Dickens and the Brontës.

ERIC RUIJSSENAARS

CHARLOTTE BRONTË'S PROMISED LAND

The Pensionnat Heger and other
Brontë places in Brussels

Selina's cover design for *Charlotte Brontë's Promised Land*

9. *Selina's illustrations*

Eric, Selina and Elle went to Brussels to join the excursion of Brontë Society members who set off from Haworth to visit the city in 1993. This was the moment when Eric decided to write his book, and it was Selina's first sight of Brussels.

Her interest in the Quartier Isabelle had been growing before that first visit. She had already met Eric and heard about his research. She had pored over his collection of maps and drawings and photos of the old streets, trying with some difficulty to match them to the descriptions in *Villette*. Her first impressions of the city were very different from her rapturous response to Haworth on her first visit there, but over the next few years, as she re-read *Villette* and learned of Charlotte's difficult but life-changing time in the city, it became important to her.

She had pored over those old maps and photos for so long that already on this first visit, walking around the streets near Bozar, the final pieces of the jigsaw puzzle were falling into place in her mind. It would not be long before she had a clear mental picture of the Pensionnat buildings and their surroundings.

The three wandered the streets of Brussels, revelling in a city that was subtly different in flavour from those of their Dutch homeland and sharing their vision of how it had been in the past. They walked and talked incessantly, sitting for hours in cafés. As Eric's research developed, Selina became increasingly involved in the visual aspects of it.

When he obtained the scholarship to do the research for his book, he asked Selina to provide illustrations recreating the Quartier as it would have looked in the 1840s. Her training as well as her visual imagination suited her to this task. Not only had she loved making models and drawing plans for buildings since childhood, but she had recently studied architecture.

With the descriptions in *Villette* and *The Professor* on the one hand and the archival material on the other, she pieced together a detailed reconstruction of the area, using her intuition to fill in any remaining blanks and uncertainties.

It was Selina's "then and now" plans of the Quartier, with the plan of the modern streets that can be superimposed on the layout of the old ones, which had guided me when I came to the bottom of the Belliard steps.

10. *Marina*

"Ce sont des Labassecouriennes*, rondes, franches, brusques"
[They are Labassecouriennes, blunt, frank, abrupt]. Mme Beck describing
Lucy's Belgian pupils (Villette, Chapter 8).

Notwithstanding Charlotte Brontë's love of the French language and contempt for the "Flemings" – a term used by her, however, to refer to Belgians in general – the first three enthusiasts I met in my quest to set up a Brontë group in Brussels were Dutch rather than French speakers.

Admittedly, Selina and Eric were from the Netherlands, and Charlotte exempted its natives from the scorn reserved for those of Belgium. She is quick to point out in *The Professor* that M. Vandenhuten, whose son is saved from drowning by William Crimsworth and who rewards Crimsworth by finding him a job, is not Belgian but Dutch. In the Belgians she can find no redeeming qualities and is often most virulent when referring to them as "Flemish".

Since the Dutch and French speakers form separate communities within Belgium geographically as well as linguistically, living in Flanders or Wallonia is like living in a separate little country within the little country that is Belgium.

Marina, the first Brontë enthusiast I met in Belgium itself, was from Flanders. I met her through the Brontë Society in connection with my proposal to start up a branch of the Society in Brussels. When she wrote to me, I was pleased to see that she worked in Rue Royale, near Lucy Snowe's park, and as her office was only a stone's throw from the site of the Isabelle quarter she offered to show me some traces of the old streets there that I had failed to find. Selina had told me that in one of these streets there was a surprise awaiting those who found themselves walking on its cobblestones. Marina knew where it was and would take me to it. Once again I found myself heading for Rue Royale in my lunch hour, stepping out of the bustling world of the European quarter into another time, into the lost world of the Quartier Isabelle and the Pensionnat.

Marina struck me initially as having some of the qualities I vaguely imagined to be national characteristics of Belgians. She appeared down-to-earth, no-nonsense, blunt. Yet I was soon to discover that under this matter-of-fact exterior beat a romantic heart. Perhaps Charlotte should have been less hasty about judging her Belgian pupils by outward appearances. In the first half-hour of our acquaintance Marina told me that one of her passions was the poetry of Emily Brontë. Another was calligraphy, and Emily's poems provided the inspiration for her designs.

In the café where we met for lunch, Marina ordered her meal in Dutch, I in French. Like Charlotte Brontë I spoke no Dutch and perceived Brussels through the medium of French. Of course I knew that Belgium was divided into two language communities but, working in an expatriate bubble, had scarcely experienced that divide myself. Brussels is in theory a bilingual city but in practice the language I heard in shops and cafés was almost always French – or English, which is increasingly becoming the lingua franca and the first foreign language of many of the more recent immigrants in the city.

Hearing Marina speak to the waitress in Dutch brought home to me that her Brussels was not the same as mine. I had already realised this with Eric and Selina. For all three, Brussels was not "Bruxelles" but "Brussel". Rue Royale was Koningstraat, Grand Place was Grote Markt. There were two parallel Brussels. Every street sign had two names on it, but since I didn't understand Dutch only the French names had fully registered with me. Charlotte had been similarly blind to the Flemish Brussels.

I asked Marina if she minded Charlotte's nasty remarks about Belgians, but she did not seem to take them personally or very seriously. It has to be said that Charlotte did not hold a monopoly on criticising people from other countries, a sport widely practised in her time and not unknown in ours!

Time and again I was to meet Belgian Brontë admirers who seemed to bear Charlotte remarkably little grudge for her remarks. Some shrugged them off with comments such as "As an English person she simply didn't understand the Belgians. I'm not sure that we do ourselves!" A Flemish novelist, Kristien Hemmerechts, even went so far as to write that however rude Charlotte had been about the inhabitants of her host country, today the feeling that was uppermost was gratification that she had mentioned them at all: "Today offence gives way to pride at this unflattering portrayal. Whatever she may have said, it is thrilling that the great English author wrote about 'us'".*

This gratitude for rudeness may seem rather extreme but in the years after that first meeting with Marina, when the project of the Brussels Brontë Group was becoming a reality, many of the Belgians I encountered cited Charlotte's most scathing remarks with humour rather than anger. A member attending one of our events who had to leave early without taking leave wrote afterwards to apologise: "Sorry for my rude, rural, Catholic, continental Labassecourian manners". A tall Flemish radio presenter interviewing a member of our group cited Robert Moore's description of a typical Fleming in Chapter 5 of *Shirley*: "'The clumsy nose standing out – the mean forehead falling back…All body and no legs…' Look at me. Am I all body and no legs?" demanded the radio journalist. In fact he was all legs!

At the time of my meeting with Marina I had already had an encounter with the Belgian assistant manager of Waterstones bookstore in Brussels. When I suggested that they stock Eric's books he agreed to do so at once. He told me that *Villette* was his favourite novel and had been the subject of his end-of-course dissertation at Leuven university.

I wonder how many managers of Waterstones stores in Britain have read *Villette*?

11. *Marina's story*

Over lunch Marina, as Selina had done before her, told me how the Brontës had become such a passion with her. She also told me how they provided inspiration for her hobby of calligraphy.

At the age of twelve she had been awarded a school prize: a Dutch translation of *Jane Eyre, Wuthering Heights* and *Agnes Grey*, all in one volume. She was especially captivated by *Wuthering Heights* and started looking for books about the Brontës in the local library in her small home town in Flanders. From between the pages of one of them fell a little piece of paper on which there was a handwritten note: "Brontë Parsonage – Haworth – Yorkshire: the Brontë home". She looked up Haworth on a map of England. She kept the bit of paper for a long time. Visiting the Brontë home became her dream.

Once she started learning English at school, she was soon reading simplified versions of English novels, the first of which was…..*Wuthering Heights*. But it was not until years later that she first had the opportunity to visit Haworth. She was working for a European trade union federation based in Brussels and was in Scarborough for a conference. After climbing up to see Anne Brontë's grave high on the cliffs there, she made her way to Haworth. The journey by train and bus took so long she had only a couple

Marina

of hours to walk round the village, but she had at last realised her childhood dream.

It was Marina's interest in calligraphy that first made her aware of Emily's poetry. When she first took it up as a hobby she learned the different scripts with their appealingly antique names – Gothic, Carolingian, Chancery. But after seeing the Book of Kells and other medieval manuscripts on her annual holiday in Ireland, Celtic script became her passion. She found it difficult. It couldn't really be taught; you had to have a feel for it and be able to invent your own designs. She gave up the classes and from then on, Emily-like, followed her own path. But she did not find her perfect subject matter until, by chance, she opened an edition of Emily's poems that had been sitting virtually unread on her shelves. It was to become her most well-thumbed book.

She told me too how *Villette* had given her a new perspective on the city where she worked. She had never liked the novel until she re-read it after coming across Eric's books. Until then she had never liked Brussels either. For years she had made the daily commute from Flanders to her office in Rue Royale near the Park without having any idea it was a five-minute walk from the site where the Brontë sisters had stayed. Like so many Belgians who work in Brussels but live in Flanders or Wallonia, those self-contained countries within a country, returning to their home towns straight after work and hardly setting foot in the capital outside office hours, she knew little about it. In her case being Flemish and perceiving Brussels as a largely French-speaking city accounted only in part for this indifference, even dislike. It seems to be Brussels' fate to be unloved, a place of work rather

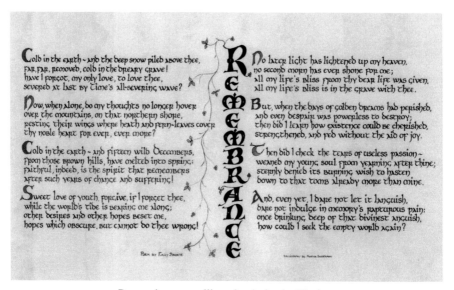

Remembrance: calligraphy design by Marina

than a place people choose to live in. Before meeting Marina I had not realised how often this dislike is felt by Belgians themselves, many of whom feel like foreigners in the city. I had assumed it to be an expatriate phenomenon; some foreigners are almost as dismissive of their adopted city as that grumpiest of expats, Charlotte Brontë.

Yet Charlotte's criticisms were directed at the people around her rather than against the city itself. The fascination it exerted over her is clear to any reader of *Villette*.

After visiting the site where Emily had spent the best part of a year – doubtless recalled with little fondness by Emily herself – and finding out more about its history, Marina began to feel more positive about Brussels. Now that she knew so much more about Place Royale and its surroundings, she saw it with new eyes. Now that she could visualise a homesick Emily Brontë wandering around the streets close to where she worked, those streets suddenly became interesting. Which just goes to show the extent to which the city we see around us is the product of our own mind, or state of mind.

12. *Rue Terarken*

After lunch Marina showed me Rue Terarken, or what remains of it, one of the few spots where you can still get a feel of the old Isabelle quarter. Like the whole of the Quartier, this street was at a lower level than Leopold II's subsequent developments and today is hidden away down a flight of steps leading from Rue Ravenstein, the street on which the main entrance to Bozar is located. At the top of the steps stands the splendid Hôtel Ravenstein, the mansion of the Cleves-Ravenstein family and possible birthplace of Anne of Cleves, much restored but one of the few buildings the Brontës would recognise today. What is left of Rue Terarken is a tiny stretch of the original street, which joined up with Rue d'Isabelle.

Rue d'Isabelle itself underwent a strange fate. Even before the Brontës' arrival, part of it, the part connected to the royal palace, had already been buried underground, when Rue Royale and Place Royale were built. The ground above it was then raised to the level of Place Royale. This severed the street's links with the palace and put an end to its proud role as a route used by the royal family. The rest of it was to disappear completely or be buried during Leopold II's redevelopment after the Brontës' time. Most curiously of all, today you can walk on the stretch that was buried first and therefore, sadly, not a bit the Brontës could have walked on. It is part of the archaeological site that has been excavated and opened to the public under the BELvue museum on Place Royale.

Hôtel Ravenstein on Rue Ravenstein, by the steps leading down to Rue Terarken

The stub of Rue Terarken that has been left, a fragment that for some reason of expediency was allowed to escape the developers' pick-axes, may have escaped interment but today it is a largely forgotten little street. Passers-by in Rue Ravenstein high above rarely glance down at it. Marina led me down to this tenacious witness to the lost world of *Villette*. Today it is a cul-de-sac, coming to an abrupt end at a back entrance to the Palais des Beaux-Arts. It is the goods entrance and the sole practical purpose of the street today is to provide a passage for vans making deliveries to Bozar. Next to this entrance was the "surprise" Selina had hinted at: a round dark-blue plaque with white lettering, an almost exact replica of those marking literary shrines all over Britain but certainly the only one of its kind in Brussels. Close scrutiny reveals that this plaque is in fact unique in the world since it has been crafted by hand. The slightly irregular white letters read:

"This plaque commemorates the old Quartier Isabelle of which the Rue Terarken is a lucky survival. Charlotte and Emily Brontë would have passed this street when going to the Pensionnat Heger in the Rue d'Isabelle where they stayed in 1842-43. The memory of this area lives on in the vivid image Charlotte portrays in her novel *Villette*."

In tiny lettering at the bottom of the plaque is inscribed a date, "May 2004", and the name "Selina Busch".

13. *The blue plaque*

Selina told me the story of her plaque. Because passers-by so often miss the one placed by the Brontë Society, she wanted to put up an unofficial memorial of her own somewhere else as a personal tribute to the Brontës. She settled on tiny Rue Terarken because it conjures up the atmosphere of the cobblestone streets the Brontës knew, as well as being secluded enough for her somewhat unorthodox project.

She took as her model the blue plaques commemorating writers' houses in Britain, so easily identifiable with their bold white lettering. Making her replica took some time and she knew that it might soon be removed by some authority or other, and that few people would chance upon it in such a forgotten street. But it was worth the effort if it introduced even a few visitors to the Brontë connection in that hidden-away bit of Brussels.

Elle accompanied her on her secret mission to place the plaque. They arrived in Brussels by train on a sunny May morning. It was around midday when they descended the steps to the diminutive street. No-one was around and they found the cul-de-sac empty of delivery vans.

The blue plaque

40

They had brought contact glue, unsure how successful this would be. Rather to their surprise the plaque stuck fast. Before departing they performed their own version of an unveiling ceremony by burning a joss stick under it and praying that it might be left long enough to be spotted by a few chance visitors. The authorities might view their act as vandalism; for them it was an act of homage.

To their surprise, the plaque was not removed. Are any of the city authorities aware of its presence? If it *has* come to their knowledge, do they care? Perhaps it has remained undisturbed because of the perennial problem of getting anything done in Brussels. The many layers of the city's administration can lead to paralysis, and matters will not have been accelerated by the long periods in which Belgium has been without a central government.

The last time I looked, the blue plaque was still there, not much the worse for wear, many years now after its secret unveiling. And the other day in a bookshop I picked up a book on memorials to writers in Brussels. I turned to "Brontë", and there was a photo of Selina's plaque in all its glory.

Rue Terarken c. 1900. The Hôtel Ravenstein is on the right
(*Brussels City Archives*)

14. *Eric's cobblestones*

Another Brontë fan from Holland, instead of leaving a token of admiration in Rue Terarken as Selina did, took a souvenir away from it, like those early pilgrims to the Parsonage who used to surreptitiously bear away something one of the sisters might have touched. There is a story of an American visitor who somehow managed to remove part of the frame and a section of the glass pane from a window in Charlotte's bedroom and use them to frame a picture in his house, so that he could view it through glass *she* had looked through.

Whether a visitor to Haworth has ever borne away a cobblestone on which the Brontës might have walked I don't know, but that was what Eric did in Brussels. He took a cobblestone from Rue Terarken, a street along which Charlotte and Emily must often have passed. Or rather, he took three stones. However, he didn't have to creep into the street one night armed with a pick-axe to acquire his memento and there was nothing illicit about it. Not long after Selina put up her plaque, he was dismayed to find that the nineteenth-century stones of Rue Terarken had been removed and the street re-paved. He wrote to the city council department responsible and asked if he could have one of the old stones as a souvenir. In the event the staff recovered three of them for him. Although they were heavy, weighing about five kilograms each, Eric bore them back to Holland in his rucksack for himself and two other souvenir-collectors. To his surprise I declined the offer of one of them. I didn't want a stone; what I sought was a literary fellowship of human beings, a Brontë literary society in Brussels.

15. *Research*

Having spent most of my working life abroad, I had never before joined a British literary society. I had now joined the Brontë Society in the hope of meeting members who lived in Belgium and bringing them together, but only Marina showed any interest in forming a local association.

Since its creation in 1893, the Brontë Society has made occasional pilgrimages to Brussels; every so often a coachload of members crosses the Channel to picnic in the park or visit the Protestant chapel where Charlotte and Emily worshipped. But Brussels is a long way from Haworth and once the coaches return to Britain thoughts of Belgium recede again until the next excursion is planned.

Increasingly, though, I thought how fitting it would be if regular Brontë meetings and events could be hosted in the city that was so pivotal to Charlotte Brontë's life.

While still pondering ways of convening the necessary band of enthusiasts, I found another outlet for my interest: assisting Eric Ruijssenaars in his continuing research interests by trying to ferret out references relating to the Brontës' stay in Brussels in old publications in the Royal Library of Belgium. For although Eric had followed up *Charlotte Brontë's Promised Land* with a second book, *The Pensionnat Revisited*, which contained new findings on the destruction of the Isabelle quarter, questions still remained unanswered and not all avenues had been fully explored.

I registered as a reader at the Royal Library on Mont des Arts off Place Royale, very close to the chapel where the sisters used to go each Sunday, with a sense of adventure. In these days of the Internet it is easy to forget the thrill of entering a big reference library. So much learning brought together in labyrinthine stores in a single building. So many index cards to thumb through in row upon row of little drawers waiting to be pulled out. In the elegant reading room in the Bibliothèque royale de Belgique/Koninklijke Bibliotheek van België, some at least of the procedures for tracking down information were still pleasingly traditional and manual.

I started what I self-importantly liked to term my "research" by hunting in 1850s Belgian journals for reviews of *Villette*. Here, I struck gold quite early on and it was with a sense of bearing off a trophy that one day I was able to take home a photocopy of a review published in 1854 in a journal called Revue *Trimestrielle*.

The review of "*Villette*, by Currer Bell"* describes it rather condescendingly as a "petit roman". The anonymous reviewer is charmed by the opening chapters set in England. For him the problems start once the action moves to Brussels. He cites Charlotte's dismissive account of everything Belgian, from the revolution in 1830 which freed the country from Dutch rule to her portrayal of the Belgian character as supposedly represented by Mme Beck and the pupils and her criticisms even of such details as the method of cleaning floors – which, Lucy informs us, was with damp coffee-grounds, "used by Labassecourien housemaids instead of tea-leaves".

In retaliation, the reviewer takes her to task over her anglicised French and choice of French expressions, in his view not just incorrect but inappropriate for the characters in whose mouths she puts them. How would she feel, he asks, if he expressed his opinion of her book in *franglais*? He gives examples: "Good gracious! Madame! Quel est ce langage? Ou avez-vous appris la speak french?"

He denies that the review is his revenge on her, while confessing that after reading *Villette* he had to wait until he felt calm enough to write a fair assessment. But despite his irritation at her mangling his language, not to speak of her attacks on his country's religion, the author is generous enough at the close of his rather amusing review to acknowledge Charlotte's qualities as a writer. As so often in Belgian reactions to the book, tolerance and humour prevail.

It is worth noting that most members of the Heger family were similarly forgiving of Charlotte's negative portrayals in *Villette*. Marion Spielmann, who was a friend of the family, reports that Heger's son Paul, reading the novel for the first time in middle age, "was amused, recognising everything…and although a little hurt by the exaggerations and unkindnesses which he rightly attributed in the main to literary exigency, he attached no great importance to that – for he realised that the book claimed to be regarded as fiction." According to Spielmann, the Hegers, who were not the only Belgians to treat Charlotte rather better than she treated them, "entertained profound respect for the writer's genius" and "were proud that her art had been first trained and nurtured within their circle".

Belgians not infrequently appear to be more annoyed by faults in her French and her use of surnames and place names than by her nationalistic prejudices. Spielmann tells us that the Hegers "were hurt that…the names of personages well known and universally esteemed in Brussels – de Hamal, van der Huten, de Bassompierre – were allotted to creations of the author's fancy", often caricatures.*

I do not know how many other Brontë enthusiasts have come upon the review in the *Revue Trimestrielle*, whether in the Belgian Royal Library or elsewhere. Others before me must surely have sat and read it in that very place, but for me it had the thrill of a discovery.

Other "research" tasks proved more challenging. One was to find out about the scandalous rumours about the Pensionnat that circulated in

Brussels after the publication of *Villette*. The novel caused trouble for the Hegers. Mme Beck's establishment was quickly identified as the Pensionnat and Mme Heger never forgave Charlotte either for her portrayal of herself or for other inconveniences and even threats to the school's reputation. One of the inconveniences was the stream of pilgrims to see the school. Unlike her husband, who rather revelled in his fame, she always refused to see these visitors. As for the potential damage to the reputation of the school, this was caused not only by rumours of possible impropriety in Heger's relationship with Charlotte but also because one of the pupils in *Villette*, the giddy flirt Ginevra, elopes with her lover Alfred de Hamal, who pays her clandestine visits through attic skylights. If the idea got about that this was based on actual events at the school, Mme Heger's Pensionnat de Demoiselles could be in trouble.

Villette and its portrayal of Mme Heger as the calculating and interfering Mme Beck was Charlotte's revenge for what she had suffered in Brussels. She probably blamed Mme Heger for her husband's failure to respond to her letters to him. However, she did try to limit the damage the novel might do by forbidding French translations of it during her lifetime. Of course her death in March 1855 followed so close on the publication of *Villette* in 1853 that there was not long to wait for the first official French translation. But even before that there were pirated ones.

I trawled in vain through Belgian newspapers from 1853 onwards in search of any whiff of the scandal concerning the school or indeed any reference to *Villette*. It is of course unlikely that such rumours would have found their way into the press.

Another possible area of investigation was what happened to the graves of Martha Taylor, a friend of the Brontës, and Julia Wheelwright, a little girl who was a pupil at the Pensionnat during their stay.

16. *Martha and Julia (I)*

Do you know this place? No, you never saw it, but you recognise the nature of these trees...the cypress, the willow, the yew. Stone crosses like these are not unfamiliar to you.... Here is the place – green sod, a grey marble headstone. Jessie sleeps below. .... [She died] in a foreign country, and the soil of that country gave Jessie a grave. (Shirley, Chapter 9).

Martha Taylor and Julia Wheelwright died of cholera within a month of each other in the autumn of 1842. Martha, who was twenty-three, was the lively and popular sister of Charlotte's great friend Mary Taylor, who had first put the idea of studying in Brussels into Charlotte's head. The two sisters were studying at the Château de Koekelberg finishing school in Brussels. Charlotte was to portray Martha as Jessie Yorke in *Shirley*, who died young and was buried in a foreign grave, describing her as "gay and chattering, arch, original...with her little piquant face, engaging prattle, and winning ways...much loved...much loving."

Julia was only seven years old, a pupil at the Pensionnat, where she was one of Emily's reluctant piano pupils, forced to take her lessons during recreation time because Emily was loath to sacrifice her study hours. She was the youngest daughter of the congenial Wheelwright family, one of the few households that the socially awkward Charlotte enjoyed visiting. Charlotte maintained a friendship all her life with Laetitia, an older sister of Julia's.

The two girls were buried in the Protestant cemetery often visited by Charlotte on her lonely walks in the countryside around the city. This cemetery, outside the town walls beyond the old gate of Porte de Louvain, disappeared in the 1870s when Brussels expanded, and some of the graves were relocated to the new city cemetery in the outlying district of Evere. Was there any chance that the girls' remains had been among those taken to Evere, and if so could their graves still be found there?

Remains had been transferred only when the families concerned had either paid for a grave in perpetuity at the time of the funeral or for a plot in the new cemetery at the time when the old one was closed. I was not aware of any record indicating that the Taylor and Wheelwright families did either of these, but further checks could doubtless be made.

But at this stage of my Brontë adventure, unfamiliar with the city and unused to delving into archives, I felt daunted by the task. Thoughts of Martha and Julia, doomed to remain in Brussels for ever after their friends and relatives had returned to England, did cross my mind from time to time and I nursed the hope that perhaps, against all odds, their final resting places were to be found somewhere in the cemetery in Evere. But thrilling

The old Protestant cemetery, Brussels
(*Illustration for The Professor by E. M. Wimperis*)

as it would be to find the graves of people long dead, I was more interested
in making contact with the living. I wanted to meet people in Brussels
today who would share my fascination with all aspects of the Brontës' stay
there.

17. *Researchers past and present*

At first, though, the only Brontë researchers in the city with whom I had any contact were dead ones.

I read about people who had done research on the Brontës in Brussels in the past. There was Marion Spielmann, a British art critic and author of *The Inner History of the Brontë-Heger Letters*, who knew the Heger family and assisted them when it was decided to donate Charlotte's letters to Heger to the British Museum in 1913. There was Frederika MacDonald, who was a pupil at the Pensionnat only sixteen years after Charlotte and Emily. Her book *The Secret of Charlotte Brontë*, which came out in 1914, the year after the letters were published, gives her analysis of Charlotte's feelings for Heger as well as her own impressions of life at the Pensionnat. Heger had been Frederika's teacher too, but she did not share Charlotte's hero-worship of him.

In the early twentieth century there was considerable interest in the Pensionnat and in every single topographical reference in *Villette*. Eric Ruijssenaars recounts* how in the 1930s Spielmann corresponded at length with two scholars, D'Arcy Thompson and Edgar de Knevett – the first a Scottish scientist and friend of Paul Heger's, the second a lawyer living in Brussels with a passion for archaeological research – concerning the exact route Lucy Snowe takes to Mme Beck's school on her first night in Brussels. (I was pleased to read that one of the streets Lucy might conceivably have passed along on her way to the Pensionnat via the park was the very Rue de la Loi that took me from my office in the European quarter to the start of my Brontë adventures in the Isabelle quarter.) Does she arrive from Ostend or some other port? Which of the city's gates does she pass through? The problem is that we can't be sure whether Charlotte had a specific route in mind. She may even be deliberately misleading the reader by mixing up her references. But the three middle-aged or elderly men disputed the question with all the enthusiasm of the excitable young girls who had picked leaves from the pear trees in the Pensionnat garden. All three were fascinated by the vanished Pensionnat, De Knevett regretting that he used to walk past it every day but never went inside. He probably spoke for many when he observed that "As often happens in life, my interest in it awoke after it was pulled down".*

And then, just as I was tiring of spending hours in libraries with dead people, I met someone of my own time who had done research on Charlotte Brontë and places associated with her in Brussels. Derek Blyth was a Scottish journalist and guidebook writer who had lived in the city for fifteen years.

18. *Derek's story*

"I have tramped about a great deal and tried to get a clearer acquaintance with the streets of Bruxelles. ...I go out and traverse [them] sometimes for hours together." (Letter from Charlotte Brontë to Emily, 2 September 1843).

Derek was quietly spoken, with a look of inward absorption and amusement. His wife was a colleague of mine but although I had met Derek through her I did not learn of his fascination in the Brontës until I read an article by him on one of his interests, Brussels cemeteries, in which he mentioned another interest: hunting out Brontë associations in the city, in this case the possible location of Martha and Julia's graves.

He had arrived in Brussels as an established guidebook writer and, like Charlotte before him, got into the habit of going for long walks in the city to get to know it thoroughly. As part of his background research he sought out works of literature with a Brussels setting. Which was how he came to read *Villette*. The introductory part of the novel didn't hold his attention, but once Lucy arrived in Brussels that changed. He was astonished by how modern the book seemed. The expatriate experience it described still struck chords in him as a foreigner living in the city in the 1990s. As he read, too, he realised that Charlotte was describing places he had seen on his walks – a church, a street, a flight of steps. The Pensionnat had disappeared, but what was surprising was that so many of the places she had known were still there. He was struck, too, by the fact that she had been living in the very heart of the city. He felt that she was not just the lonely figure in a foreign city she is usually perceived to be, that she revelled in its art, literature and music and was inspired by it.

He was interested in the importance of Brussels in *Villette*. It is much more than a background to the novel; it gives the story its shape. Wherever Lucy goes in the city – whether she's descending some steps, entering a church or wandering along a street – everything around her takes on significance.

With his guidebook writer's nose for places and their associations, he found himself drawn into the game of trying to identify the places referred to in *Villette*. It is a guessing game Charlotte forces us to play as soon as we start trying to trace the real places she had in mind, for whereas in *The Professor* Rue d'Isabelle is Rue d'Isabelle, in *Villette* real places are disguised by fictitious names, often facetious and disparaging. Belgium is Labassecour (farmyard/poultry-yard), Brussels is of course *Villette*, little town. Charlotte changes the names of the city gates through which Lucy passes on her walks to the Protestant cemetery or in her carriage rides with

Dr John Bretton and his mother. Lucy refers to La Terrasse, the Brettons' little "château" or manor house, as being a mile beyond the "Porte de Crécy"; since there was no such gate in Brussels we can only speculate about the direction in which the château lay, assuming it was based on a real place she had seen. Crécy is the name of a battle that was victorious for the English. Is it a veiled reference to Waterloo? Did Charlotte mean by it that La Terrasse lay in the direction of Waterloo? Derek wanted to find out if he could.

Quite a lot of research had already been done on the Pensionnat (unknown to Derek, Eric Ruijssenaars was already working on his contribution to this research; before it came out, Derek sometimes thought of writing a "Brontë places in Brussels" book of his own) but not everything was known about other places mentioned in *Villette*, or the Brontës' friends and acquaintances in Brussels.

In her novels Charlotte rarely invented her fictional places, but based them on locations she knew, for example friends' houses. Of course she must have changed and combined some places, as suggested by the confusion regarding Lucy's route to the Pensionnat on the night of her arrival. But generally speaking, in both *The Professor* and *Villette*, the latter written a decade after her Brussels years, she seems to have retained a photographic memory of the city's streets and buildings. Many have been identified but questions remain. What about Rue des Mages, where the priest who hears Lucy's confession lives? Or Faubourg Clotilde where M. Paul rents the little house for her school?

These questions would recur to Derek at regular intervals during his ramblings in Brussels garnering facts for his guide books. From time to time he sought answers in the city archives.

The archives are located in a building formerly occupied by a textile wholesale company in the "Marolles" district, today a lively, ethnically diverse area around Gare de Midi and the city's famous flea market. The building has been preserved intact and you sign yourself in at the wooden counter on which curtain lengths used to be cut from rolls of material for local ladies.

In this slightly odd place, Derek would search for clues to some of the places described by Lucy Snowe – places that have long disappeared; for example, none of the houses proposed as La Terrasse are still standing today.

It would be interesting to know how many Brontë enthusiasts before him have done such research while actually living in Brussels.

Over the years he had other projects too. The tourist authorities had never done much to make visitors aware of the Brontë connection, let alone organised regular Brontë walks. Derek devised a tour which became a chapter in his book of Brussels walks, *Brussels for Pleasure*, published in the same year (2003) as Eric's second book on the Isabelle quarter. (The two of them had been pursuing the same interest. The Scot and the Dutch-

Entrance hall of the Brussels City Archives
(*Photo: Myriam Devriendt*)

Derek

man might have bumped into each other in the archives or on the site of Rue d'Isabelle, two thoughtful rather dreamy men, without either having any idea of what the other was up to.)

Derek had the idea of organising regular guided Brontë walks, along the lines of the James Joyce literary walks in Dublin (though with fewer stops at pubs). But he was discouraged by the thought of the bureaucratic hurdles that might be placed in his way. It wasn't until the birth of the Brussels Brontë Group that he guided his first walk, as a private activity for members.

Another project was even more ambitious. To the best of his knowledge no feature film had ever been made of *Villette* (a 1970 BBC adaptation has been lost to posterity). But surely it was a novel crying out to be filmed. He worked on a screenplay, over the years approached producers and directors about the project, and would amuse himself by picking out suitable actresses to play Lucy.

When I met him, none of these projects had yet been fully realised and he still had many unanswered questions, but he didn't seem to mind. He enjoyed guessing games and projects that existed only in his head. Charlotte continued to tease him with her cryptic topographical references, and her time in Brussels, which had been so deeply significant to her, continued to fascinate him. As for Charlotte herself, he found her sharp, rather intimidating (might Emily have been the more appealing of the two sisters?) but always interesting. As the years went by she began to haunt him a little. Sometimes, walking in the city, he was almost aware of her as a tantalising presence, close to him in its streets.

19. *I go to Haworth at last*

While I was still wondering about the best way of locating other Brontë enthusiasts in Brussels in order to form a literary association there, I paid my first visit to Haworth over the weekend of the Brontë Society's 2006 annual get-together. I was to see the Parsonage for the first time and find out what it was like to be one of the members of a literary society coming together around a common passion.

Most Brontë fans immerse themselves in Haworth and its moors before perhaps, years later, managing a flying visit to Brussels – a weekend at most – to have a quick look round the sites there. For me it was the reverse experience. Although the Brontës had been familiar to me since my teenage years, I had never visited Haworth. It was partly lack of opportunity but also a certain reluctance lest the real place should fall short of the one I had always pictured so vividly.

If I had wished to have the Parsonage and the moors to myself and wander about them with my musings uninterrupted, I had chosen one of the worst weekends of the year. At the beginning of June each year, dozens of Brontë Society members congregate in Haworth to listen to talks, sit in the church where Patrick preached for forty years and walk in the places trodden by his children during their brief lives.

However, apart from the fact that my interest was in literary societies and their members as much as in literary shrines, I did not feel any particular need for silence and solitude in order to get close to the Brontës in Haworth. I had felt close to them since I was twelve. Through the years I had pictured them in the Parsonage, talking, writing, peeling potatoes. I did not really expect any new intensity of communion with them in Haworth. That intensity belonged to my first childhood encounter with Jane and Rochester and with the Charlotte of Mrs Gaskell's *Life*, who had been with me ever since, and more recently with Lucy Snowe.

Many first-time visitors to Haworth – Derek, for one – report their impressions of a harsh, bleak, grim, flinty, dark and rainy place. My first impressions were much more benign. By arriving at midsummer, with the prospect of finding the place full of people who shared my interest in its literary associations, I no doubt denied myself what is perceived to be the authentic "Haworth experience".

Before the other members descended on the village I did at least have some moments of solitude. I arrived well ahead of the weekend's events and when I walked up Main Street for the first time one mild June evening the day trippers had gone home and I was alone for my first sighting of the outside of the Parsonage. It did not disappoint me, but seeing the Brontës' home as an adult could not be as thrilling as reading their novels or life stories as a teenager. It was the same when I walked through the rooms of the house the following morning. The place had been more vivid in my imagination, peopled by the living Brontës, than it was as a museum to them.

The vanished Pensionnat, precisely because it had vanished and had to be reconstructed in imagination, had taken on a life in my mind in a way the real-life Parsonage could not, precisely because it had been preserved.

The Pensionnat, despite all she suffered there, remained tremendously important to Charlotte Brontë because it was the place where she fell in love. The Parsonage, although a much-loved home in some periods of her life, was also to become a place that oppressed her with the memories of those who had shared it with her and were there no longer, a place from which she fled increasingly as depression set in after her siblings' deaths. In the lonely years when she was writing *Villette*, she fled in imagination from the Parsonage to return to the Pensionnat and to Brussels.

Charlotte evokes places brilliantly in her novels but in real life they were perhaps not as important to her in themselves as they were to Emily, who was never happy away from Haworth. The Parsonage was a beloved place to Charlotte only when she was happy there with her brother and sisters, and again with her husband in the last year of her life. The Pensionnat was fascinating to her chiefly because she had lived there in hourly expectation of seeing Heger. It was people that mattered most to Charlotte.

But whatever the Parsonage meant to her, today it draws visitors from all over the world, including the Brontë Society members I was now to encounter. I wanted to know what kind of people join literary societies. Would they be like those in Stevie Davies' novel *Four Dreamers and Emily* about attendees at a conference in Haworth – people who turned to the Brontës because of loss, loneliness, dissatisfaction with their own lives, and whose interest in the literary family often became obsessive? People like Eileen Nussey, convinced she's a descendant of Charlotte's friend Ellen Nussey and that only she understands the nature of "passion" as found in the Brontë novels, or Timothy, the lonely widower who is visited by Emily's ghost?

Over the weekend I did encounter a handful of people with bees in their bonnets, for example the lady convinced she was a descendant of an illegitimate child of Branwell Brontë. She saw a strong resemblance between her profile and Branwell's and the lack of definitive proof of the existence of such a child had not shaken her faith or deterred her from doing a great deal of genealogical research. Or the man who was often conscious of Charlotte's presence, who not infrequently saw ghosts of all kinds, in fact. I heard of a lady who, while taking a photograph of the Parsonage, asked Charlotte to give her some sort of sign that her spirit was present; when the photo was developed, a dark shadow in the doorway appeared to some to be the silhouette of a woman in the full-skirted dress

Main Street, Haworth

of the mid-nineteenth century. I met a lady connected with the Nussey family who, among other memorabilia, had inherited a photo she was convinced was a hitherto unknown one of Charlotte Brontë, although many were equally convinced it was of Ellen Nussey.

Yes, literary societies and the Brontë Society in particular have their share of dreamers and visionaries and people convinced they are in possession of unique insights into their literary idols, however unusual their theories may be. But in fact what struck me most about the people I met over the weekend was their sheer diversity rather than the proportion of eccentrics. Many of them in fact seemed to be "ordinary" people who had simply felt a closer connection with the Brontës and a greater fascination in their lives than the average reader. A lot of these were down-to-earth Yorkshire people who felt pride in the county's most famous writers. Some had an encyclopaedic knowledge of every place ever visited by a Brontë. But there were also enthusiasts from the other side of the globe whose knowledge was equally encyclopaedic. The journal *Brontë Studies* is kept well supplied with a steady flow of articles.

The endless reworking of "the Brontë myth" can be dismissed as an industry, a commercial ploy which ensures that visitors continue to flock to the Parsonage and that academics and film producers are kept in business. But it does lead people to the books. And it is the power of the books themselves and of their authors' lives that continues to grip the imagination of each new generation.

More even than the events organised over the weekend, the talks and the walks to Top Withens, I relished the evenings in the Old White Lion listening to the tales of other Brontë Society members. Everyone had a story to tell. Their own life story, and how they had been enriched by their literary interests. Colourful events and personalities in the annals of the Society over the years. Thoughts about the Brontës' books and lives, from speculation about the tantalising gaps in our knowledge of the family (did Emily write a second novel and if so, did Charlotte destroy it?) to discussion of the prose legacy Emily did leave to us, that most disconcerting of novels, *Wuthering Heights*.

Before my visit to Haworth, non-Brontë enthusiasts had quizzed me sceptically about the Society and its annual weekend. What, they wanted to know, could there possibly be to say about the Brontës that hadn't been said before?

Admittedly much of the research, the lectures, the new biographies and fictional accounts that come out in a steady stream, are simply the re-telling of a much-told tale. But the appetite for hearing it appears to remain inexhaustible. Listening to the animated talk in the Old White Lion I realised that the story of the Brontës' lives and the stories of the characters they created, like all enduring fairy tales and myths, do not become any less satisfying because they are told again and again, and that each person who hears them, and each generation, will interpret them in their own way.

So on the train back to Brussels I thought not just of the moors of Haworth but about the conversations with other members. I wondered whether it would be possible to create a similar group in Brussels, and whether one of the *tavernes* in Grand Place would one day be the setting for the kind of evenings I had enjoyed in the lounge bar of the Old White Lion.

20. *The birth of the group*

During my stay in Haworth I had experienced a pleasure new to me. Added to the enjoyment given me by the Brontës themselves I now had that of meeting a group of people who were drawn together by a common interest in them, who had things to say to one another. I was more and more attracted by the idea of bringing people together around the theme of the Brontës in Brussels.

In Haworth I had met two people who were interested in the Brussels project. One was Marcia Zaaijer, an archivist from Rotterdam. The other also lived in the Netherlands but was Dutch only by adoption. Maureen Peeck O'Toole had been born in Bradford, but after marrying a Dutchman and moving to Holland had taught English literature at the University of Utrecht until her retirement. Until she went abroad she took the moors and Haworth for granted. But when you leave your home country you become more aware of your background, your culture, even your language. It was after leaving Yorkshire that she began to take a greater interest in the Brontës. She often lectured on their work to her Dutch students.

Maureen was a friend of Eric's. She had assisted and encouraged him when he was writing his books.

No sooner had I returned from Haworth than the Brontë Society put me in touch with two women in Brussels itself, not known to each other, who had both approached the Society to ask if there was a branch in the city. Sheila Richardson had lived there for thirty years but it was only recently, now her children were grown up and she had more time to herself, that she had really become aware of her adopted city as a place where the Brontës had lived. Sheila Fordham had only just arrived to take up a post but was already finding she did not take easily to living abroad. Previously she had worked with foreign students at Leeds University. She recognised in Charlotte and Emily's problems in adapting to life abroad the phenomenon – today known as "culture shock" – that she had observed in these students and was now experiencing herself!

Apart from myself, therefore, there were now Eric the researcher, Selina the artist, Marina the calligrapher, Derek the journalist, Maureen the academic, Marcia the archivist, Brussels veteran Sheila Richardson, and Brussels newcomer and culture shock expert (and sufferer) Sheila Fordham. Elle, whose enthusiasm had created momentum for the project before it was dreamed of, was not there and I was not to meet her for some years. At a meeting of the nine of us in my sitting room in the autumn of 2006, the idea of the Brussels Brontë Group became a reality.

Most of the Dutch members already knew one another but many of the others were meeting for the first time. There was a sense of many paths converging, of a coming together of enthusiasts who had pursued and been changed by their literary interests in different ways. Maureen Peeck had written her thesis on Emily's poetry, so one way in which she had approached the Brontës had been the analytical one of literary criticism. Sheila Fordham was particularly interested in their lives, which often served as a reference illuminating her own; since her arrival in Brussels she found herself wondering how they must have felt there, drawing comparisons. But for everyone present, as is usually the case with a writer you feel close to, the Brontës had in one way or another been companions over the years.

Marcia told us about her first encounter with them. One evening she was in the local library with her mother. She was looking for an adventure or mystery story. Her mother told her to hurry because they were expecting a visit from Marcia's uncle. He was her favourite uncle – a sea captain with a fund of exciting stories – so she grabbed the first book she saw with the word "*mysterie*" on it and they hurried home.

She happened to have seized upon the very book that set Elle on the trail of the Brontës around the same period, Johan van der Woude's *Het mysterie van de Brontës*. Perhaps it wasn't surprising; at the time there weren't that many books about the family in Dutch.

The book triggered Marcia's interest in the Brontës and from then on she felt a sense of familiarity whenever she encountered them. They kept reappearing in her life, her path seemed to cross theirs again and again. She felt that things were always leading her back to them. In the words of another book about them that she read, "There is always a connection."

Sheila Richardson told us about her love of *Wuthering Heights*, instilled in her in childhood by her mother, and how as a busy mother herself, packing for the summer holidays, the last item on her list would be a book for herself, something easy to read and satisfying. For some years *Wuthering Heights* was often thrown hurriedly into her case and never disappointed her. One year she read it three times. She told us, too, how *Villette* also had a special place in her family. As a young man her father had worked as a travel guide in the summer holidays. One year, when based in Brussels, he fell in love with a young woman in his party. "The rest, as they say," Sheila told us, "is history". The young woman was her mother. The city where her parents met was to become Sheila's home, and it was her mother's love of the Brontës and interest in *Villette* because of her own Brussels love story that led Sheila to our group.

At this first meeting, Eric and Derek met for the first time and realised they had started researching Brontë places in Brussels at around the same time, fifteen years earlier. In the intervening years, both had visited cemeteries to look at Heger's grave or speculate about those of Martha Taylor and Julia Wheelwright. Both had pored over old maps of the Isabelle quarter in the city archives and pondered the exact location of the Château de Koekelberg, Mary and Martha Taylor's boarding school.

Derek had read Eric's books and now told him about his own Brontë projects and dreams. The book he had begun, which was still unfinished. His idea of starting up guided walks; his dream of organising a *Villette* exhibition in Bozar on the site of the Pensionnat or a concert of the music Charlotte heard in the park and describes in the novel; the screenplay for *Villette* he was mentally drafting.

This first meeting brought another new pleasure which must be one of the main satisfactions of forming any association: that of bringing together like-minded enthusiasts who would not have met otherwise. It is fun to meet kindred spirits through a network but even more gratifying to be involved in actually spinning the web of that network.

21. *The website*

We were convinced that there must be many more people in Brussels interested in the Brontës, and at this first meeting we discussed the best ways of alerting them to the existence of our embryo group. One of the most valuable suggestions to come out of the meeting was that we create a website for the group. Although lovers of nineteenth-century literature are not always remarkable for their computer literacy, one of our number volunteered to undertake the task. Selina offered to place her artistic talents at the service of the project and learn the skills needed to design the website.

We could – at some expense – have employed a professional for the purpose, but it is unlikely that the result, however competently executed, would have been as vivid and personal as the website Selina finally came up with. The fact that she was learning as she went along, building up her creation slowly and laboriously, made it highly individual.

She embarked on the task with no knowledge of web design and only a basic knowledge of computers; she owned one but was the complete opposite of a computer geek, being the kind of person who got far more satisfaction from sending a friend a letter exquisitely hand-written on pretty notepaper than from the instant gratification of an e-mail exchange.

She was self-taught and set up the site with the aid of a manual and some technical hints from a brother. The first few weeks were more hard labour than creative fervour. But once the technicalities had been mastered, the project became even more creative than illustrating Eric's books. She wanted the site not just to tell people about our group and the Brontës in Brussels but to be visually exciting, to entice visitors into the world of *Villette*.

Panoramic view of Brussels, 1905. Picture postcard showing the Isabelle Quarter,
with the Pensionnat on the far right
(*Dexia Bank postcard collection*)

Visually, the site was inspired by a panoramic view of Brussels from a photo on an old postcard, with the Cathedral on the skyline and the Pensionnat in the foreground. This image of the old city, its soft mauve-greys brightened by the warm splash of the red tiled rooftops, the grey spires of Sainte-Gudule rising against a pink sky, became the background for the website's pages.

As our group was soon to do, the website rapidly took on a life and momentum of its own. The edifice grew day by day as Selina created pages within pages, Chinese-box style, with links leading you further into particular aspects of the story, inviting you to wander down the alleys and byways of old Brussels.

New pages could always be added. One of these explored Emily's, as distinct from Charlotte's, experience of Brussels. According to Charlotte, Emily never felt comfortable abroad and "was never happy till she carried her hard-won knowledge back to the remote English village, the old parsonage-house, and desolate Yorkshire hills".* We can only speculate as to the exact nature of the influence of her continental stay – but how interesting it is to speculate!

Other sections look at the historical background and the figures belonging to it – Waterloo and Wellington, of course, but also Belgian independence, won in the Revolution of 1830 in which Heger is reputed to have fought, and Leopold I, the first king of the newly formed country.

The site was intended to have something for everyone, introducing newcomers to the story while also providing a resource centre for scholars. Eric's research was the basis for the scholarly information, while Selina contributed plans and images from Brussels archives.

The result of her labours was a vivid and visual website, her response to the intensity of the world created by Charlotte Brontë in *Villette*. Each click of the mouse draws you further into that world. The Pensionnat and its garden fired Charlotte's imagination. Her creation, *Villette*, in turn fires the imagination of readers like Selina, and Selina's rendering of Charlotte's vision fires that of visitors to the site. It draws them down the Belliard steps to Rue d'Isabelle, through the door of the lost Pensionnat, along the paths of its vanished garden.

The Blog

Someone suggested we should start a blog as well as a website. A blog? Some of us, old fogeys, wrinkled up our noses at first. We barely knew what the word meant, being more at home browsing in second-hand bookshops than on literary forums online. However, the blog was set up, and became a complete record of the group's activities and its members' projects.

Thus, ironically, a group formed to share an interest in the literature and history of the past introduced some of us to a technology of the present and

Nineteenth-century trinket box with picture of Sainte-Gudule, image used on the website
(*Brontë Parsonage Museum*)

overcame our prejudices against it. Although I am still happy to live without Facebook and Twitter, I am fully reconciled to the equally unappealingly named invention of the blog. Nothing quite equals the satisfaction of reading a newsletter in print on paper and holding it in your hands, but our blog has proved to be an attractive and efficient means of sharing a passion and recording all the stages of a joint project.

22. *Birthday celebration*

The website was launched just in time for our first event. We were ambitious and wanted to invite speakers and organise talks as well as tea parties at one another's houses. For this we needed a lot more people. We started by advertising a weekend in April 2007 to celebrate Charlotte Brontë's birthday on 21 April.

We were joined by a handful of members from the Brontë Society's London branch who represented some of the diversity of the Society's membership. Jerry had been a Thames waterman, a modern counterpart of the ones who rowed Charlotte out to the Ostend packet one January night when she returned to Brussels in 1843. Val was a jazz singer and Brenda a university teacher.

Brussels weather can usually be relied on to be unreliable – wetter or colder or hotter for the time of year than can reasonably be expected. On this occasion it was hotter, an early heat wave, and it was a happy weekend, an auspicious beginning for our venture. We lunched in the rooftop restaurant of the Art Nouveau Musical Instruments Museum overlooking Place Royale; the panoramic view of the city used on our website was taken from this vantage point at the top of what was then the Old England department store. The white columns and dome of St Jacques-sur-Coudenberg, whose bells Charlotte could hear from the Pensionnat garden, glinted in the sun, as did the park bandstand – another landmark she would recognise today.

Derek led the first of what were to become our regular guided walks. It proved to be unique in our annals because of the unexpected presence of a resident in the city with an interest in history and archaeology who added his own, unscheduled, commentary to Derek's and provided proof that the Brontës do not attract eccentrics only in Haworth. The conclusion of each part of Derek's commentary marked the beginning of a long and digressive discourse by our mysterious visitor just as we were preparing to move on. Whereas Derek's remarks clarified and explained, the mystery man's left us increasingly bemused as the walk progressed. While our thoughts were of Charlotte and her forbidden love for the married M. Heger, he spoke of amorous liaisons between priests and nuns in convents in the Isabelle area, of conspiracy theories and of ecclesiastical, archaeological and amatory matters to which he believed *Villette* provided clues. We never saw him again and some of us have since wondered whether he was a vision, a ghost. His presence was somehow fitting, providing the atmosphere of the obsessive and supernatural prone to hover around anything connected with the creators of *Wuthering Heights* and *Villette*, and which evidently pervades the site of the Pensionnat as well as Top Withens or Haworth Parsonage.

Place Royale, 1843
In the centre is the church of St Jacques-sur-Coudenberg
(*Royal Library of Belgium*).

Thoughts of ghosts also crossed our minds when, after our walk had concluded at the Cathedral, the scene of Charlotte's confession's, we adjourned for tea in a meeting room on the first floor of a well-known bar, a venerable establishment whose name also denotes one of Brussels' best-known beers, *A La Mort Subite*. For our tea party marking the anniversary of Charlotte Brontë's birth we had ordered a cake decorated with the words *Happy Birthday, Charlotte*. A waiter, tall, solemn, and formally dressed in the splendid uniform of Brussels waiters, bore it into the room where we sat expectantly and asked: "Which one of you is Charlotte?"

23. *Torrent of passion*

The next step was to make our group known in Brussels by opening up our events to the wider public. Derek was to give a talk, the first lecture organised by us.

He chose as his subject Charlotte's letters to M. Heger – the despairing SOSs sent from the Parsonage to the Pensionnat after her return to England.

Derek had always wanted to see and hold the originals. Armed with a letter of recommendation from the Brontë Society, he took the Eurostar to London and paid a visit to the British Library. Having procured a reader's pass and wearing the mandatory white gloves, he was at last able to handle the four letters. Three of them were at some stage torn up; one of them also suffered the indignity of being used by Heger to scribble a note about his bootmaker.

One of Charlotte Brontë's letters to M. Heger which was torn up and then repaired

According to the account given in old age by Heger's daughter Louise ("Georgette" in *Villette*) to Marion Spielmann, the English friend of the Hegers who arranged for the donation of the letters to the British Museum,* three of the letters were torn into pieces by Heger and retrieved from the wastepaper basket by his wife, who glued or stitched them together again and then hid them away. Why did she go to all this trouble? According to Spielmann, who is reporting what Louise was told by her mother, Mme Heger feared that Charlotte's obsession with Heger might drive her to do something to harm the family in some way. She kept the letters in case evidence should be needed of the true nature of the relations between her husband and his ex-pupil, in other words to show that he had been blameless. If, as Louise claimed, the letters were torn up and rescued as soon as they were received, when Charlotte was still unknown, no-one could have had an inkling at that time of their future importance in revealing the emotions of a world-famous author.

According to Spielmann's report, when Louise showed the letters to her father after her mother's death, fifty years after they were written, he threw them away a second time and they were once again retrieved – this time by Louise. It is thus a miracle that they have survived to be read by us today.

Back in Brussels, Derek tore a sheet of notepaper into eight pieces and laboriously sewed them together again in order to time the operation. It took him two hours.

For this first talk organised by the group we had found rather an odd venue. The cost of hiring most lecture rooms was at that time beyond our means and this one was cheap, a meeting room in a Bohemian restaurant in the old city centre that organised arts events. It was pleasantly lined with books but too small and the lighting was unaccountably dim – perhaps because it was primarily used for slide shows.

Over fifty people sat crammed into this room in the semi-darkness on the evening of 18 October 2007. We had advertised the talk widely and our group had caught the imagination of the media. *Agenda*, the Brussels *"What's On"*, wondered whether a Brontë craze might be imminent on a par with the current Austen mania, and advised *Bruxellois* to be "one step ahead of the pack" by going to the talk: "Close your eyes and let yourself be swept along by this torrent of passion in the life of a future literary bestseller". The lack of lighting meant there was hardly any need for the listeners to close their eyes.

Whether these first attendees were swept along by a torrent of passion I don't know, but Derek brought a refreshing enthusiasm to his subject. He was a journalist, not a seasoned expert on the Brontë lecture circuit. He spoke of the unanswered questions in the Heger letters saga, the elements of an unsolved detective story. He had the excitement of someone who had pursued his Brontë interests outside the mainstream of Brontë studies and was for the first time sharing it with a group of other enthusiasts, on an equal footing.

He had recently been told a ghost story that would have been familiar to Brontë Society habitués but not to those of us gathered in the dark little room in Brussels. He had heard it from a keeper of manuscripts at the British Library, whom he had met in Ghent at an exhibition of British art to which she had travelled with the manuscript of *Alice in Wonderland*. The story was about something that happened to a curator from the Library who was bringing back a Charlotte Brontë manuscript from Haworth. He took a taxi from King's Cross to the Library. When he got out of the cab with the manuscript the driver asked him what had happened to "the lady". "What lady?" he asked. And the driver said: "The little lady in grey who was sitting next to you".

Derek told us how, when exploring Brussels, he had at times been similarly aware of the presence of that little figure in grey.

24. *The reading group*

Derek's talk had brought our group to the attention of the Belgian media for the first time, and they seemed intrigued and slightly perplexed by our antics. A reporter from the Flemish newspaper *De Standaard* referred to the formation of the first Belgian branch of the Brontë Society as "a craze blown across the Channel from Britain to Brussels – people who meet to talk about the works of the Brontë sisters".

Another rather more recent craze is the vogue for reading groups, of which there are many in Brussels, mostly meeting to discuss contemporary novels. Our next group venture was to found one devoted solely to the nineteenth century. The first book on our list was *The Professor*, but we did not confine ourselves to the Brontës.

Most book clubs meet either in pubs and cafés or in people's houses. The problem is that the former are noisy while the latter offer too much temptation to chat aimlessly or gorge on the provisions provided by the hostess. To avoid both these evils we asked the sympathetic management at Waterstones, whose deputy manager was so keen on *Villette*, if we could hold our meetings somewhere in the store, and they offered us their staff room high up in the labyrinthine offices at the top of a dark stairway.

The building is an historic one in the Brussels literary scene, having housed an English bookshop since the early twentieth century. For decades, before it was Waterstones, it was a W.H. Smith store in whose cafeteria the foreign and Belgian bourgeoisie of the city would refresh themselves after shopping at Marks & Spencer's in nearby Rue Neuve. During the German occupation in the Second World War the building was requisitioned by the Nazis, who used the maze of back offices as a headquarters and officers' mess.

As so often in the history of our group, the warm welcome extended to us went a long way towards making up for the city's former tendency to cold-shoulder the Brontës. The manager and deputy manager bent over backwards to accommodate us. Members who successfully negotiated the security locks giving access to the back stairs up to the top floor would find a little book display set out on the table and an invitation to help ourselves to coffee. The perpetually cheerful and seemingly workaholic manager would stay on late in her office on the evenings of our meetings until it was time for us to make the long descent down several flights of stairs to the tradesmen's door, the store having closed some time before, a descent sometimes performed in pitch darkness because the light switched itself off before we reached the bottom. All this provided a unique backdrop and atmosphere for those first reading group evenings, evoking thoughts of the Nazi boots that must have clattered up and down the steep wooden steps in the war years.

The reading group

Our group must be one of the most multinational book clubs in the world. Many of its members work at EU institutions, hurrying from their computers and PowerPoint presentations in office buildings in the European quarter to discuss Thackeray, Dickens and Jane Austen. Some are British or Irish but they are just as likely to be Swedish, Portuguese or Bulgarian. Whether or not they have studied English Literature at university, and some have, they are often as well versed in the English classics as comparable native speakers of the language. Years after its first beginnings, this little band of people from all the countries of Europe, coming together in its capital – people who first read the works of English literature in their youth in Finnish and Romanian and Greek – are still meeting monthly to share impressions of the English classics of the nineteenth century.

25. *The growth of the group*

Thanks to our website and the advertising of our events, the Brussels Brontë Group had taken off and from now on it grew rapidly, mushrooming from the little knot of nine people who first met in my sitting room to fifty, then a hundred and more in the space of just a few years. Our members were of all ages as well as all nationalities, from young trainees to people who had retired to the city to be near offspring working there.

In Britain, where literary societies seem to have limited appeal for the under-sixties, they face dwindling and ageing membership and would doubtless be delighted to experience a similar boom in their numbers. It has to be said that our success was not solely attributable to hard work, since certain aspects of life in Brussels helped the growth of our little group. In any city with a large expatriate population there is a captive audience for cultural activities. Expats gravitate towards events organised by other expats, where they can see familiar faces as well as make new friends.

As an expatriate, too, you find yourself joining in activities you might never think of trying in your homeland. Play readings, toastmasters clubs to improve your speaking skills, country dancing, book clubs galore.... It's on offer in your language and perhaps one of your friends is doing it. Why not give it a whirl?

A talk on the Brontës? You don't know much about them but you read *Jane Eyre* years ago. You decide to give it a go. There are sure to be familiar faces there, people you've met through your other leisure pursuits – your theatre group or choir....

In most European cities you might expect activities in English to be dominated by native speakers of the language. Less so in Brussels, where there are so many different nationalities and English is the one language common to all. For foreign anglophiles, a talk on the Brontës can be viewed as an opportunity to practise the language as well as to refresh their knowledge of the English literature studied at school or university.

Another reason for the popularity of our group was the ease with which its events could be advertised. The word can be spread rapidly in a city where so many work for an international organisation or delegation of some kind.

You're organising an event that you think will appeal to the Irish community in Brussels. How can you reach them? Nothing easier. Your friend Mary works at the Irish embassy (or is it the Permanent Representation of Ireland to the EU?). She can advertise your event there, and mention it to her boss, the ambassador. If you think the Northern Irish community will be interested you can send an e-mail to Rose, who's a secretary at the Office of the Northern Ireland Executive in Brussels, which represents the region to the EU institutions. You can also talk to your friend

Tom who's the treasurer of the Irish Club of Brussels, your colleague Patrick who's in the Irish Theatre Group, or John who's involved in organising the St Patrick's Day Parade.

The British community has forums such as the "Brussels British Community Association". I once had an example of how certain concerns of its more traditional members appear to have remained unchanged since Brontë or even pre-Brontë times. Items on the agenda for its AGM included the Duchess of Richmond's ball, Waterloo and the Duke of Wellington. For a moment I thought I must be back in 1815. The Duchess of Richmond's Ball, described in Thackeray's *Vanity Fair*, was held in Brussels on the eve of Waterloo and officers were summoned from it to the battlefield. Wellington was of course the victor of Waterloo – and hero of Charlotte Brontë. But why were British residents of Brussels still discussing these matters in the twenty-first century? Because there is still an annual Duchess of Richmond's Ball to commemorate the events of 1815, because the present Duke of Wellington is one of its sponsors, and because plans were under way for events to mark the 200th anniversary of the battle.

Despite the help given by "networking", however, the chief reason for the success of the group is the drawing power of the Brontës themselves. Among other novelists, only Jane Austen commands a similar following, but there is no comparable interest in her life story.

Brontë enthusiasts in Brussels, as elsewhere, no doubt, are journalists, secretaries, artists, teachers, musicians, students, interpreters, IT experts, people working for every conceivable kind of company, consultancy, NGO.

"I've loved the Brontës since reading *Wuthering Heights* as a teenager...." "I have been working here for two years and have only just learned that the Brontë sisters lived here for a time. I'd like to know more and visit the places they saw."

One lady had worked in the city for decades and had always assumed that the places described in *Villette* were imaginary until a visiting friend asked her to track down the location of the Pensionnat. To her amazement she realised that the site was within a few yards of an office building she had worked in for years. She had often ascended the Belliard steps on her way to run in the park at lunchtime.

One Brontë fan who had just stumbled on the connection wrote hopefully: "Anne is my favourite of the sisters. Did she come to Brussels too?"

Paula, an American art historian, wrote: "After going on one of your walks I became fascinated by how the Brontës' personal story connected with the urban development of Brussels." Her interest in the Brontës was awakened long before her move to Brussels. *Wuthering Heights* had such a powerful effect on her as a teenager that she spent an entire summer trying to write a similar novel of raging passion. Her own novel was abandoned but the impact of Emily's remained with her. When she came to find out about the sisters' lives, being herself the daughter of a small-town clergyman was one reason for identifying with them.

Oscar, from Galicia in northern Spain, a rural region of mists and ghost stories, was also a fan of *Wuthering Heights*, whose landscape reminded him of his homeland. He was interested to learn that two girls who grew up in such an environment also experienced continental and cosmopolitan life and culture.

Everyone finds their own connection with a favourite author. Do people find more diverse links with the Brontës than with other writers? The many points of connection, whether with the poetry, the moorland settings, the passionate heroes and independent-minded heroines of their fiction or their real-life struggles and tragedies, are first forged in the teens but are often strengthened and deepened at each reading as an adult.

Our group is a point of convergence for people who were led to the Brontës in their youth, a first encounter which usually had a lasting influence, and whose paths have later led them to Brussels.

Members of the group moving on to pastures new after a stint in the capital write to tell us how much they enjoyed the hours taken out of their busy time here to explore Brontë byways with like-minded people.

The pleasure of exchanging impressions about books is perhaps the main *raison d'être* of all literary societies. Reading is necessarily a solitary pastime but such societies transform our experience of literature into a shared one. Any common interest will draw people together, but books and writers seem to create a particularly fertile ground for discussion. Exploring insights into favourite books with others is a good starting point for exchanging life experiences and perspectives. An added dimension in the Brussels group is that literature provides a common ground for people from such a diversity of cultures.

The Brussels Brontë connection also draws people from outside the city. Paul, who is British, had worked in Maastricht for much of his working life and often visited Brussels, an easy train ride away, returning home with a case full of booty picked up in the city's wonderful second-hand bookshops. On each visit he wondered whether there was anything still to be seen of the places described in *Villette*. One day he decided that on his next trip he would go and look for them. In preparation, he googled "Brussels" and "Brontë" and was taken straight to our website. On our next guided walk, he was there, and in the ensuing discussion in a café in Place Royale found himself talking about *Villette*, that expat novel, with people who were foreigners abroad like him and who knew their Brussels and their Brontës intimately. He had seen the site of the Pensionnat at last – and the discovery had been shared with others. Along with the second-hand books, he took home with him a warm memory of the day spent sharing literary passions with a group of Brussels expatriates in Place Royale.

26. *Liviu*

Our group did not only attract foreigners comfortably established in jobs in Brussels. The power of the Brontës' novels also drew into our midst people in the city who were outside that cosy circle.

Charlotte and Emily never intended to stay long in Brussels and some of today's expats, too, spend only a brief spell in the city, taking up temporary posts here before moving on. But it is also a city of immigrants, who come with the intention of making new lives in it.

Liviu's path crossed ours for only nine brief months, but throughout that time he was an assiduous member of the group. Tiring of ill-paid jobs in his native country, he had come to Brussels in search of work. But despite drive and ability, his attempts to find stable employment came to nothing, and our Brontë gatherings must have been bright spots in a period of failure and frustration.

He never missed one of our events unless prevented from doing so by one of the menial jobs he had to take to keep body and soul together. He always took care, too, to be among the members who went for a drink with the speaker after a talk. Nursing a single drink for hours, he would get as close to the speaker as possible, and not just to listen. He was never happier than when engaged in eyeball-to-eyeball intellectual conversation.

After each event he would e-mail to say in his perfect English how much it had meant to him.

He had a look of intensity about him that marked him out as being different. I think he did feel set apart in some way. Despite the frustrations of his time in Brussels you sensed that he retained a belief in himself. He told us that reading the Brontës as a teenager was a revelation, and their genius inspired him to try and realise his own powers. He had read the novels just after the Romanian revolution. His was an ordinary working class family, but there were books in the house, and among them were *Wuthering Heights* and *Jane Eyre*. The Brontës were well known in Romania and would have been in many families' book collections. He felt that Romanian sensibilities were particularly drawn to the intensity and depth of feeling of Romantic literature.

It was in Brussels that he first became interested in the Brontës as people. He remembered reading somewhere that they had lived in the city, and now he found out that like him they had gone there in the hope of improving their job prospects. After that he started reading more about their lives. He couldn't afford to buy books while in Belgium and didn't even fulfil the requirements for joining a library, but he read everything he could online.

Initially he liked Brussels, but as he became disillusioned by his experiences there he started to view it in a darker light.

Liviu

We saw him for the last time shortly before his departure from Brussels; he was giving up the struggle and returning to a job in his own country. He told us that knowing about Charlotte and Emily's foreign adventure meant he would always remember certain streets as being associated with them. In Charlotte's disappointment and depression during her stay he found some parallels with his own; it added poignancy to the sadness of his time in the city.

27. *The homeless lady*

At one of our events we were joined by a lady who explained that she did not have enough money to pay the entrance charge. Her garb, and the flowers in her hand, declared that she was a member of the least fortunate class of immigrant, one of the city's large contingent of *personnes sans domicile fixe*. We waived the fee and she sat at the back. After the talk there were questions for the speaker. As always, it was an articulate audience with plenty to say. About fifteen minutes into this discussion phase, the lady at the back rose to her feet and spoke wildly and at length.

A year or two passed without any further sign of her, but a couple of weeks before a talk we had scheduled on *Jane Eyre* I received an e-mail. "Madame, I am a social worker at SAMU [*an organisation that helps the homeless*] and am writing to you on behalf of Madame ..., who is in a shelter where I work. Madame would like to attend your event and talk about Jane Eyre, whom she loves very much, but she is in a difficult situation and doesn't know if she can afford it."

The day came, and the homeless lady appeared again, a bunch of white flowers in her hand. She deposited a large pile of small coins on the table. As before, we assured her that we would waive the entrance charge for her. She sat at the back again and I wondered uneasily how to cut her short tactfully if she got up and spoke for as long as on the previous occasion. Discussion time came, with no shortage of questions and comments from the confident Brussels audience, but the homeless lady remained silent. I took a last question, feeling relieved. Then the speaker said "I think that lady at the back wants to say something."

"I'm afraid we'll have to call it a day now," I said hastily. Immediately I felt mean and guilty.

So as people began to leave I had a few words with the lady. She was hovering near the door with her flowers. I asked why she admired Jane Eyre and she spoke for some time but I didn't really understand much of what she said. The difficulty was in following her train of thought rather than in understanding her English.

As she turned to go she laid a flower on the table. "For Jane".

As soon as the door closed behind her I felt dissatisfied with myself. Could I not have made more effort to bridge the gap between our worlds – the mental gap which seemed to yawn as wide as the material one – and to explore what it was that had brought her to this room, in a city in which we were both immigrants?

This woman was homeless. Jane Eyre knew what it was to be homeless. Jane Eyre knew what it was to be an outsider and so did this woman. But I suspected I was drawing over-facile parallels based on the label "homeless person". Probably Charlotte Brontë's novel exhilarated and consoled this

Brontë enthusiast for much the same reasons as it did the rest of us.

I still wish, though, that I had found out more about how the germ of that interest first started to grow in her, and what exactly Jane Eyre meant to that woman in a shelter for the homeless in Brussels.

28. *Messages*

Apart from the Brussels inhabitants who continually join the group, thanks to our website we are contacted by e-mail by people from all over the world. Hardly a week passes without someone approaching us on the most diverse subjects.

One week it may be a message from a descendant of a fellow pupil of Charlotte's and Emily's at the Pensionnat, interested in researching their ancestor. Another, some query on a point of detail about which we are sometimes as much in the dark as the questioner. One correspondent wanted to know whether Charlotte's letters to Heger were torn up and sewn together again before or after he showed them to Mrs Gaskell, who would surely have been very surprised by the sight of the repaired letters. If they were torn up as soon as Heger received them, Mrs Gaskell must indeed have seen them after they were repaired, unless he simply read them out to her. Given that Heger was able to lay his hands on them during Gaskell's visit, Louise Heger's account cannot have been strictly accurate, since she claimed that after retrieving the letters Mme Heger hid them away for fifty years.

Some messages are unusual to say the least, like the one from a gentleman who claimed to be descended from an illegitimate child of Heger's with "either Charlotte or Emily Brontë", and complained bitterly that he had been trying in vain for years to convince the Brontë Society of the truth of his story.

Many of them are from students seeking information on the Brontës' Brussels stay in relation to dissertations or theses. Some make the journey here, eager to locate any traces of the Brontës still to be found in the capital. A Spanish mature student prepared her visit so thoroughly she even wrote to the Cathedral to ask if they had a register of Charlotte's confession. An Italian student wasn't sure whether the Pensionnat was still standing. Either that, or she was simply reluctant to accept its disappearance, asking us hopefully: "Can I find the school of Emily and Charlotte?"

I wish she could. I wish I could take her to the top of the Belliard steps, wave a magic wand and conjure up a vision of it all for her as it was in 1842: Isabelle quarter, street, school and garden. I can only hope that she and all such visitors find the school in their minds and succeed in wandering along the Allée Défendue in imagination, and don't just feel the pang of disillusion when they look down the steps at the prospect that meets their eyes today.

As for the graduate student who wrote to the Cathedral, one wonders about the reaction of the staff when asked if they have a record of Charlotte Brontë's visit there one September afternoon over a century and a half ago. Almost 170 years after her brief half hour in a Sainte-Gudule confessional

Population register for 1842 with Charlotte and Emily Brontë's names
as inmates of the Pensionnat Heger
(*Brussels City Archives*)

at a moment of low ebb, the interest felt by some in every event of her life is such that they long to be shown some document with her name on it, something tangible to look at and hold.

Luckily for them there is such a document in Brussels, though not in the Cathedral. In the city archives you can see the population census for 1842 and there in the list of inhabitants at No 32 Rue d'Isabelle are Charlotte and Emily Brontë, spelt "Bronti".

The most enthusiastic messages we receive are from young Brontë fans. An English schoolgirl staying in Brussels for a few days with her mother e-mailed from their hotel. She was a "massive fan" of the Brontës. Could I tell her where the sites were? I sent directions but heard nothing further until I received a thank-you message over a year later, apologising for getting back to me rather late but reporting success in following my instructions.

Among Brontë-mad students there are many Americans, as in the days when Adeline Trafton and her friends sought out the Pensionnat. For these far-flung readers, setting foot at last in the spots where Jane Austen or Charlotte Brontë walked before them – so far from their home country but so often seen by them in imagination – is an exciting adventure.

Beth, a twenty-two-year-old American student on a "literary pilgrimage" to Europe, wrote from Dorchester to ask for directions to the Brussels Brontë places. Having "done" Haworth she was now doing Hardy's Wessex one day and Charlotte Brontë's Villette the next, travelling overnight from south-west England to Brussels by coach. She said it was because of the Brontës she was studying literature and told me how thrilling it was to be in the places that had inspired the works she had studied.

These messages thrill me in turn with the sense that the literature of the past can still excite the young of the twenty-first century. When we see young people absorbed in images on screens – though nowadays their parents are just as likely to be engaged in the same pursuits – it is easy to assume that their generation can have little interest in communing with nineteenth-century writers. Their chief concern appears to be instant and continual communication with their peers via a keyboard. Had I glimpsed Beth hunched over her laptop or Smartphone on the coach to Brussels, I would have thought her an unlikely reader of *Villette*. I would not have suspected that she was in fact writing up her blog about her literary tour or texting a friend to tell her breathlessly how "awesome" it was going to be to stand on the site of Lucy Snowe's Pensionnat.

29. *From conference interpreter to Brontë guide*

*A miscellaneous assortment they were...I had under my eye French,
English, Belgians, Austrians, and Prussians. (Crimsworth describing his
pupils in The Professor, Chapter 12).*

*Villette is a cosmopolitan city, and in this school were girls of almost
every European nation (Villette, Chapter 9).*

*The gentleman...politely accosted me in very good English...I wished to
God that I could speak French as well...It was my first experience of that
skill in living languages I afterwards found to be so general in Brussels.
(Crimsworth reporting one of his first conversations with a Belgian in
The Professor, Chapter 7).*

Charlotte Brontë thought a lot about language while she was in Brussels.
She came to improve her French and learn some German and, like all
language learners and foreign residents abroad, must have spent much time
mentally translating: translating to herself the French she heard, and
translating into French what she wanted to say to those around her. In her
essays for Heger she tried to express her thoughts correctly in his language,
though inevitably in her own somewhat anglicised version; I have often
heard criticism of the French dialogue in *Villette* by Belgians, who
complain that Charlotte or her publisher should have had it revised by a
native speaker. But then it would not have had the idiosyncrasy of her own
utterance. Native French speakers are always hard on those who attempt to
speak their language. Her linguistic skills were impressive considering that
she had only schoolgirl French when she arrived in Belgium and spent less
than two years in the country.

Today it is impossible to live in the Babel that is Brussels – officially a
bilingual capital and moreover one full of foreigners speaking every
European tongue – without thinking constantly about languages. In 2008,
a central Brussels library held a one-day conference on the theme of "Les
Soeurs Brontë à Bruxelles", in which we collaborated. Each district in the
city has separate libraries for French and Dutch speakers. This library is a
francophone one so their talks are usually in French. Since on this occasion
there were talks in English as well and not everyone in the audience
understood both languages, simultaneous translation was provided from
French into English and vice versa.

The conference was introduced by the Mayor of Brussels, Freddy
Thielemans, who switched effortlessly between French and flawless
English – the latter, oddly enough, with a slight cockney accent – with a
few sentences in Dutch thrown in for good measure. He told us he was glad
that the Brontës had had the good taste to come to Belgium to learn French,

a humorous reference to the fact that Belgian French is not considered to be the purest, an opinion echoed by Charlotte herself in references to the Belgian accent.

In the coffee break I chatted to Myriam, one of the interpreters, a francophone Belgian. She taught English language and literature to trainee interpreters and was well acquainted with the Brontës' works but until the conference had not been aware of their Brussels connection, despite having worked in the city all her life.

She now realised that she had missed an opportunity of engaging her students. Many had been more attracted by the story of the Brontë family and the Yorkshire background than by the novels themselves. It would have tickled their fancy to know that the streets of Brussels also featured in the Brontë story. She could have taken them to the Belliard steps and told them all about the sisters' stay in their capital.

Myriam was vivacious, dynamic and funny, throwing herself into whatever interest was uppermost with her. She soon became a leading light of the group. She signed up for an OU English literature course and dreamed of one day writing a thesis on the Brontës.

The first person to lead our guided Brontë walks, Derek, was too busy to do so regularly so Myriam offered to be our tour guide and spent a summer working up her commentary, in the process learning much about her native city. Her discovery of its link with the Brontës gave her a new perspective on its history.

Myriam
(*Photo: Paula Cagli*)

30. *The guided walks*

As far as I am aware, regular Brontë tours had never been a feature of Brussels before our group initiated them. No doubt many people had toyed with the idea over the years, like Derek Blyth, who had included a Brontë walk in his book *Brussels for Pleasure*.

The enthusiasts who signed up for our first walks led by Derek had the honour of being guided round the site of the Pensionnat by a man who over the years has written many guidebooks to Belgium. But as the walks became more popular we needed more guides. Myriam was the first person to step into the breach.

It might seem that too little remains of the Brussels the Brontës knew to make for an interesting tour, but of course part of the appeal of the Pensionnat is precisely that it has vanished yet lives on so vividly in the pages of *The Professor* and *Villette*. If it had been preserved as a museum like the Parsonage, today it would probably be sandwiched between a Carrefour Express and an EXKI self-service restaurant in a Rue d'Isabelle changed beyond recognition.

What is in fact surprising is that so much of what the Brontës knew remains today. The Pensionnat and the Isabelle quarter have gone and so has the hotel near the stagecoach terminus where the Brontës spent their first night in the city, not far from the school on a site that is today close to Gare Centrale. But we still have the statue of General Belliard erected ten years before the Brontës' visit, just after the Belgian revolution against the Dutch. A French general who had fought for Napoleon, he supported the Belgian revolt. A couple of years later, while walking through the park from the palace, he died of a heart attack close to the spot where his statue now stands. His last days had been dedicated to the Belgian cause.

We have, too, the Belliard steps. Although today's steps are not the original ones, their descent to the lower level of the Pensionnat site aids our virtual immersion in the world of *Villette*. There is also the white and gold Chapelle Royale, still an important place of worship for Belgian Protestants and in the Brontës' time attended by the Protestant King Leopold I of Belgium. It nestles in the graceful sweep of the secluded Place du Musée hidden away behind the great art galleries on Place Royale. There is Place Royale itself. Wellington stayed in one of its classical white mansions, while another housed Edward Brown's bookshop and circulating library for the city's British community in the decades after Waterloo. Did Charlotte and Emily ever borrow books there? There is Rue Royale where Charlotte glimpsed Queen Victoria in a carriage with her uncle Leopold I, and the Cathedral where Charlotte and Lucy Snowe knelt at one of the confessionals.

And of course there is the Park where Wellington, asked on the eve of Waterloo whether he thought he would win the coming battle, pointed to a

Chapelle Royale today. The Chapel is in the crescent-shaped building in the centre
(*Photo: Selina Busch*)

Chapelle Royale and Place du Musée in 1844
(*Brussels City Archives*)

British soldier strolling under the trees and replied that the outcome depended on whether "he had enough of that article". Charlotte too must sometimes have walked here, since she describes it so hauntingly in *Villette*.

The tour also includes some remnants of old Brussels, survivors of the Isabelle quarter – tiny Rue Terarken and the equally old Rue Villa Hermosa, and the stretch of Rue d'Isabelle itself that has been preserved underground under Place Royale and can be accessed via the BELvue museum.

The guided walks quickly became popular. Participants are both Belgian and foreign, people new to the city and long-term residents.

The walk brings to life a bit of Brussels whose history is often unknown to both visitors and residents even though it lies at the heart of one of the most visited tourist areas. The tour covers little more than the immediate surroundings of Place Royale, and involves more standing and listening to the guide than actual walking. But although so much has to be imagined rather than seen, with the aid of old engravings and photos and street maps participants carry away some vivid associations.

"I don't feel as I've been in Brussels at all. I seem to have been in another place altogether", said one lady after the two-hour tour. She had lived in the city for decades.

Some people clearly become caught up in the story of Charlotte and Heger. An Italian trainee spending a few months in the city abandoned a walk before the end because of heavy rain. She e-mailed later that day: "Due to the rain I missed the final revelation.... Did Charlotte have a love affair with the Professor?"

31. *The American journalist*

We soon had a second volunteer guide to alternate with Myriam. Jones Hayden was an American who'd been working in Brussels for about ten years.

Jones and his family came to Brussels when he was offered a job there as a financial journalist. He and his wife fell in love with the city. Shortly after moving there he read *Villette* and Derek Blyth's book of Brussels walks, *Brussels for Pleasure*. Thanks to Derek's Brontë walk he traced the places described in *Villette*, never imagining that one day he would be leading a Brontë tour himself.

For Jones, the charm of finding out about the Brontës' stay in Brussels was the sense of having made a discovery, something revealed only to a chosen few. Everyone knows about *Jane Eyre* and *Wuthering Heights* and Haworth and the Brontës' tragic lives. Far fewer have read *Villette* and fewer still realise that the sisters actually stayed in Brussels. He felt he knew something special about them not shared by the mass of general readers or viewers of the many film adaptations.

As an American in Brussels, this feeling was enhanced by the lack of knowledge of many of his compatriots back home about the city, which in the USA is one of the least known European capitals. He had found himself there by a chance turn in his career and then discovered that Charlotte and Emily had ended up there in a similarly fortuitous way.

Jones
(*Photo: Paula Cagli*)

A Brontë guided walk. The group are at the top of Mont des Arts

He had never guided before and was a little nervous before leading his first walk, on which the participants were American, Belgian, British, Bulgarian, French, Irish, Polish and Russian. But he found he very much enjoyed interacting with them. On each walk he re-worked his commentary a little; there was always new material to incorporate, a fresh angle to take. Sometimes, on a visit to London, he would sign up for tours by the learned and loquacious guides who conjure up a bit of Victorian London or lead their mainly American customers into nooks and crannies buried away in the City of London that have survived the bombs of the Second World War as testimony to the world known to Samuel Pepys or Dr Johnson. He would return to Brussels with new ideas for the Brontë walks, which bring back to life a part of the city that underwent as complete a destruction at the hands of the city fathers who should have protected it as parts of London from enemy bombs.

By recreating the Brontës' stay in Brussels and transmitting his interest in it to others, he had found a creative outlet for that interest.

It seems fitting to have an American guide steering people around those literary sites. In the nineteenth century and up to the time of its demolition in 1910, many of the most enthusiastic literary tourists or pilgrims who came to Brussels to seek Charlotte Brontë's Pensionnat were American. The excited teenage girls who knew chunks of *Villette* by heart and were in love with M. Paul were almost always from the USA, stopping off in Brussels as part of their European tour, eager to see Lucy Snowe's school. Now, a hundred years after its demolition, an American is guiding multinational groups of twenty-first century enthusiasts around the site of the vanished school.

32. *The archivist: correcting myths and errors*

Our guided walks cover the immediate environs of the Pensionnat site and have many sources of information to draw on. But there are other places in Brussels with Brontë associations which are less well documented, as Derek Blyth soon realised when he tried to identify some of the locations in *Villette*.

One of the things that never ceased to surprise me was just how many Brontë enthusiasts I came across in Brussels, and among them was a quiet Irishman who like two other quiet men – Eric the Dutchman and Derek the Scot – had been haunting the city's archives for years in search of answers to some of the unanswered questions about these sites.

Brian Bracken worked as an archivist at an EU institution. But his passion was local history and this was to lead to his zeal in unearthing new facts relating to the Brontës' stay in Brussels. One day he bought Eric Ruijssenaars' book on the Pensionnat at a Brussels bookstore. It ignited a latent interest in the Brontës, whose books he had always liked. As an Irishman he found a connection with them in their Irishness – the fact that their story began with Patrick Brunty of Drumballyroney and ended with Charlotte's widower Arthur Nicholls in Banagher. (But despite her ancestry Charlotte seems to have had it in for the Irish as well as the Belgians, to judge from her remarks about Lucy Snowe's predecessor, the nursemaid Mrs Sweeny).

From the start, Brian's interest was in the more obscure Brontë connections in Brussels, such as one of the facts most difficult to establish – what was the model for La Terrasse, the Brettons' "quiet little château" or manor house on the outskirts of the city where Lucy finds a haven after her confession in the Cathedral and subsequent nervous collapse? Various theories have been mooted. Charlotte Brontë usually had real places in mind in her descriptions, despite the fact that the scenes set at La Terrasse have a fairytale unreality about them, with Graham Bretton as the handsome prince and Mrs Bretton as fairy godmother.

Nearer to hand, there were places close to where Brian lived that had connections with the Brontës, places he passed by every day. Chaussée d'Ixelles, for instance, where they used to go for Sunday lunch in the house of the Reverend Evan Jenkins and his family, the scene of some desperately uncomfortable meals owing to the sisters' taciturnity.

There were also still things to find out about the Pensionnat despite all that had been written about it. The first time he went to the city archives to find documents relating to the Brontës' stay, he sought out the list of all the inhabitants at 32 Rue d'Isabelle in the 1842 census drawn up in March of that year. There were the Hegers, and there were Charlotte and Emily Brontë ("Bronti"), who had arrived the month before. The books containing the census registers are kept in the reading room. It was exciting to lift down and open the huge, heavy volume containing the page with their names on it, exquisitely penned in the neatly-ruled columns.

All the boarding pupils at the Pensionnat are listed. They include an Irish one – not mentioned by biographers as far as Brian knew. Trying to find out more about the Brontës' fellow pupils would become one of the abstruse avenues of research along which he took some exploratory rambles.

He was struck by how little interest there had been in Belgium in *Villette* and how little research had been done by Belgian scholars on the places featured in it. Brian was something of a conspiracy theorist and suspected a conspiracy of silence against the novel which to some degree continues today. Was it only because of Charlotte's criticisms of Belgium? Yet Baudelaire and other visitors to Brussels were equally scathing. Was Charlotte also disliked because she was a woman, and an intelligent one?

When the Brontës in Brussels *were* mentioned in books written in Belgium, myths and errors were often perpetuated, ranging from minor inaccuracies to legends, which can still be found in books coming out today, such as the claim that Charlotte returned to Brussels at least once in the 1850s and wrote part of *Villette* in Grand Place!

Errors and myths could have crept into information on the Hegers as well as the Brontës. Brian questioned and cross-checked everything before accepting it as fact. Did Heger's jeweller father really go bankrupt after making a rash loan to a friend in need, supposedly the reason why there was no money for Heger to become a lawyer as originally planned? If he did, why was his shop still listed in a commercial register two years after he died? Did Heger really fight in the Belgian revolution of 1830? Was there evidence for this?

Tracking down the Brontës in Brussels was a good research project for someone with the patience to verify such points of detail. The Brontës have always been surrounded by myths and mysteries and speculation, and Brussels is no exception.

Brian comes from Dublin, from James Joyce country. Every place mentioned in Ulysses has been traced and written about ad nauseam. With *Villette* and Brussels the opposite is true. So much remains to be investigated.

33. *Where was the Jenkinses' house?*

The Reverend Evan Jenkins, the brother of a clerical friend of Patrick Brontë's in Yorkshire, was chaplain to the Protestant Leopold I and took services at the Chapelle Royale where Charlotte and Emily worshipped. It was his wife who recommended the Heger school to them. He and his family stayed on in Brussels, and his sons became British chaplains after him.

Brian's research on the exact location of the Jenkinses' house is an example of how inaccuracies can creep in and be passed on from biographer to biographer. Sometimes this is due to errors in the original sources. An address often given for the house is Chaussée d'Ixelles 304, the number cited in Winifred Gérin's biography of Charlotte. However, Brian found that Gérin was using an erroneous address listed in an 1840 register of Brussels addresses called the *Indicateur Belge*. In registers for other years and in the population census the address is given as Chaussée d'Ixelles 388.

Approximate location of the Jenkinses' house in Chaussée d'Ixelles. This house, with its Brontë associations, may have stood on the site of the shoe shop called Pronti!

Today, however, that number does not exist. Chaussée d'Ixelles, now a very long street, ends at No 359! The explanation, Brian found, was that the system of street numbering changed completely shortly after the Brontës left Brussels and before the Reverend Evan Jenkins died in 1849. He sought out Mr Jenkins's death certificate, on which the street number was entered as No 138. He was then able to locate this number almost exactly in census registers and maps of the period. There have been minor changes in numbering over the years but he worked out that the site of the house must be close to where No 138 stands today.

A trivial detail. Few people would have the patience to put in the work needed to establish it. Few would care enough to do so. But somehow it is oddly satisfying – and not just to an archivist – to have even such a minor inaccuracy corrected. It is satisfying to see what can be done by an investigator on the spot, familiar with the sources and with time to look at them. To know something, however trivial, that previous biographers, with all their knowledge, did not, something they simply didn't have the leisure to verify. To know that there are people like Brian, passionate enough about a subject and about hunting down information in the interests of accuracy to bring something like this to light. And to be able to stand on the spot where we now know the Brontës' walk would have ended each Sunday, in Chaussée d'Ixelles, today a crowded shopping street. Whenever I stand in such a place in the Brussels of today, there is always a feeling of incongruity and surprise at the thought that the Brontës were here.

34. *Charlotte Brontë's Ungrateful Rat*

Brian was thus steadily building up a body of scholarship on the Brussels Brontë connection. But valuable as his finds were in Brontë circles, none of them had yet prompted world headlines.

However, one day in February 2012 this quiet researcher, arriving at work for another routine day at the office, opened his e-mail inbox to find a clutch of messages very different from those usually awaiting him. *The Guardian, The Telegraph, The Daily Mail* – the British dailies were tumbling over one another to be the first with a scoop on a Brontë discovery by one "Brian Bracken, a Brussels-based archivist". Journalists from other countries round the world had also got wind of the story. A little later that morning the phone calls began. Radio 4's World at One wanted an interview. The BBC World Service asked him to go to their Brussels studio.

In fact this sudden media interest did not come as a complete surprise to him. A few months previously he had made a chance discovery that he knew would cause something of a stir, but he had anticipated neither the timing nor the force of the storm in which he now found himself. *The London Review of Books* was due to publish an article on his find the following week, on 8 March 2012, but had put it on their website much sooner than he expected, and the story had immediately been taken up by other newspapers worldwide.

> "Charlotte Brontë's lost short story for tutor to be published." "Lost Brontë manuscript rediscovered in Belgian museum."

Brian had by chance stumbled on something all literary scholars dream of, an unpublished manuscript. He owed his discovery to a brother of Constantin Heger's called Vital.

For some time Brian had been doing extensive research on Constantin. One day in July 2011 he was browsing through the electronic catalogue of the Musée Royal de Mariemont in southern Belgium on the off-chance of finding a mention of Vital Heger, who was at one time a representative of the Tournai tapestry and carpet factory not far from Mariemont; the museum's vast and eclectic collection includes tapestries. He didn't find what he was looking for, but in his search for carpets his eye was caught by the names "Heger" and then "Charlotte Brontë".

The catalogue showed the first words of a manuscript in French with Charlotte's name on it which appeared to form part of several papers donated by Paul Heger:

> Un Rat, las de la vie des villes, et des cours.... [A rat, weary of the life of cities, and of courts...]

"Un rat" caught his eye. He couldn't remember reading anything of Charlotte's about a rat.

The manuscript had a title, *L'Ingratitude*. Could it be a *devoir* (homework assignment) for M. Heger? He did some checks and found a mention of it in Mrs Chadwick's book *In the Footsteps of the Brontës*, published in 1914, as one of the devoirs at that time in the possession of Paul Heger. It was mentioned again, this time as "untraceable", in a list of Charlotte's early manuscripts drawn up in 1924. And it was not in the collected edition of the *devoirs* brought out by Sue Lonoff in 1996.

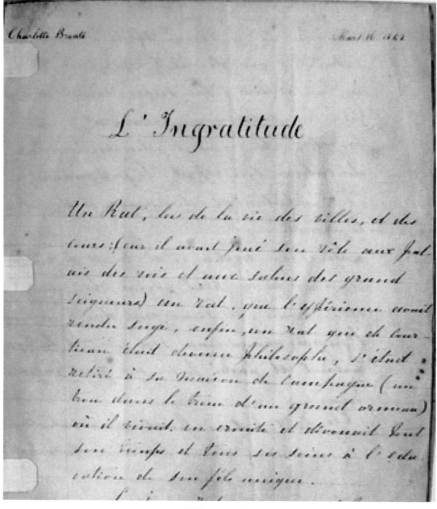

L'Ingratitude
(*courtesy of the Musée Royal de Mariemont*)

He would have to make more checks to be sure that this really was a 'lost' manuscript, but the first step was to go to the museum to see for himself whether it was an original or a facsimile.

The Mariemont museum, built in the 1970s, stands in what is now a public park in the midst of the flat countryside and drab, straggling towns of a former mining area near Charleroi. It contains the collection of Raoul Warocqué, a wealthy coal magnate and obsessive collector who owned the château which formerly stood on the site. Although the countryside could not be more different from the hills and moors of Yorkshire, there is a parallel between Warocqué's mansion and those of the Yorkshire mill-owners known to the Brontës, dotted around a landscape blighted by the industries that created their wealth. In 1960 the château suffered the same fate as Thornfield Hall.

The well-looked-after museum is quiet. There seemed to be more staff than visitors on the day of Brian's visit. Although uninspiring from the outside it is a pleasant building to wander in, with restful views of the surrounding lawns. Access to the Brontë manuscript did not involve any of the formalities Derek had encountered at the British Library – the form-filling, the white gloves. An appointment to view it was all that was required. The curator led him into a library which is a replica of the one in the former château. The gold-tooled books lining the walls are the original volumes; when the building burned down, the whole of Warocqué's collection, housed in an annex, was saved from the flames, including Charlotte's manuscript.

It turned out that her little *devoir* is just one of the items in an album of mementoes relating to Charlotte and the Hegers. The album itself, made of brown card, is plain enough, but as the curator turned the pages for him in the dimly-lit library Brian saw that there was much in it of interest. Together with *L'Ingratitude*, written on ruled exercise-book sheets, are facsimiles of the four letters from Charlotte to Heger now in the British Library, some 1913 newspaper articles reporting the publication of the letters, and several letters from Paul Heger to Raoul Warocqué which tell the story of how the manuscript came to be in Warocqué's collection.

After hearing of the publication of Charlotte's letters, Warocqué had asked his old friend Paul Heger for something in her handwriting for his manuscript collection. Heger wanted to please Warocqué, who had given generously to his university. The Heger family did not have any other letters of Charlotte's but his sisters found this essay of hers, one of those kept by Constantin. The other items assembled by Paul, which included photos of the Pensionnat, made up an attractive gift.

Warocqué had to wait a little for his present. Heger promised him the manuscript in 1913 but did not send it until 1915, one of the excuses given by him for the delay being the little matter of the outbreak of the first world war.

After seeing the manuscript Brian no longer had any doubt that it was an original. But further investigation was needed to be sure that some other library didn't have a copy or that it hadn't already been published, perhaps in an out-of-print book or catalogue.

Having established that it was indeed an unpublished *devoir*, he didn't publicise his find at once. He wanted first to do more research into the circumstances under which the essay had been acquired by Warocqué, and the literary sources of Charlotte's little fable. In the months that passed before his article was ready for the London Review of Books he kept quiet about his discovery, disclosing it only to a couple of fellow scholars sworn to secrecy. When the media storm broke he felt uneasy both at being in the limelight and at the newspaper headlines' focus on Charlotte's "love for her married teacher". It was something of a relief when the reporters moved on and he could get back to his previous research.

The interest in Charlotte's feelings for Heger echoed the headlines in the 1913 press cuttings in Paul Heger's album. But the imagination of the press was also caught by the manuscript itself, by Charlotte's sad and moving little story of an ungrateful young rat who abandons his home and a caring father in search of excitement, and perishes in the attempt. The tale ends on a startlingly bleak, almost brutal note.

When she wrote the fable, Charlotte, too, had just left a loving home in search of new experience. She too was to suffer in consequence, though her own fate was less dramatic than the young rat's. She herself was destined to return to the nest, which she continued to find unbearably confining at times, to suffer much heartache as a result of her foray into the world, but ultimately to emerge enriched from it.

The tale, however, was written at a time when she could not have foreseen her later unhappiness. It is dated 16 March 1842, only a month after her arrival at the Pensionnat, when she was in the first flush of enthusiasm for Brussels.

Why did the *devoir* not come to light earlier? One reason is that the museum's collection was not catalogued electronically until a few years before Brian spotted it online. Another is that the staff may well have assumed that its existence was already known by Brontë scholars. And it is perhaps understandable that the curators of a vast collection of nearly 6,000 manuscripts whose authors include Erasmus, Galileo and Mozart did not realise the interest that would be excited by a French homework exercise.

In December 2011, a few months before the publication of Brian's article in the *London Review of Books*, one of Charlotte's tiny juvenile manuscripts was sold by auction to a Paris museum. At the time it was thought to be the first and only Brontë manuscript in a European museum. It is an odd coincidence that the very same year had seen Brian's discovery of a lost Brontë manuscript that had slumbered for a hundred years in a library in the south of Belgium.

35. *Martha and Julia (II)*

*But, Jessie, I will write about you no more. This is an autumn evening, wet
and wild. ...[It] reminds me too forcibly of another evening some years
ago: a howling, rainy autumn evening too – when certain who had that
day performed a pilgrimage to a grave new-made...sat near a wood-fire
on the hearth of a foreign dwelling. They were merry and social, but they
each knew that a gap, never to be filled, had been made in their circle.
They knew they had lost something whose absence could never be quite
atoned for so long as they lived... . The fire warmed them; Life and
Friendship yet blessed them; but Jessie lay cold, coffined, solitary – only
the sod screening her from the storm. (Shirley, Chapter 23).*

One piece of research no-one had yet got round to completing was the
question of the graves of Martha Taylor and Julia Wheelwright.

Evidently, Martha is the one who interests us most. All we know about
seven-year-old Julia is that she was a pupil at the Pensionnat, that Emily
gave her and two of her sisters piano lessons much against their inclination,
and that Charlotte was fond of the Wheelwright family, who returned her
affection although none of them could stand Emily.

Martha, the younger sister of Mary Taylor, one of Charlotte's two best
friends, is also a minor figure in the Brontë saga, but she comes vividly to
life in the first extant letter of Charlotte's written in Brussels, to her other
old school friend Ellen Nussey.* This letter was in fact a joint production
composed by Charlotte with Mary and Martha Taylor on a visit by the
Brontë sisters, three months into their stay in Brussels, to Château de
Koekelberg, the Taylor girls' boarding school to the north of the city. It was
to stand out as a happy day for Charlotte, already feeling homesick. Clearly
the two Taylor sisters, who wrote most of the letter, did not share her
tendency to depression. They bubble over with high spirits, and although
they laugh at the oddities of the other inmates of their school they do so in
a spirit of fun, without any of the sourness of Charlotte's descriptions of her
own schoolfellows and teachers.

The Château de Koekelberg school resembled the Brussels of today in
being a mix of nationalities and a cacophony of languages. Teachers and
girls were a mixture of Belgian, English, French and German. Attempting
to learn French and German, and surrounded by people speaking languages
not their own with amusing results as idiomatic expressions were rendered
literally in other tongues, Martha complained that "in attempting to acquire
other languages I have almost forgotten the little I knew of my own".

One of Martha's brothers, Joseph, who often travelled between Yorkshire and the continent on business, had accompanied the Brontë sisters and
their father to Brussels and was to be a lifelong friend of Charlotte's. He

The Château de Koekelberg school in 1887

may have delivered this letter to Ellen, and Martha playfully instructs Ellen to pull his hair for her the next time she sees him.

Apart from her reincarnation as Jessie Yorke in *Shirley*, Martha thus flashes into life whenever we glimpse her in this and earlier letters from Charlotte. But just over six months later she was dead of cholera, as was little Julia.

36. *The site of the old Protestant cemetery*

Charlotte often visited their graves on her long, solitary walks. It is no longer possible to do so today. The Protestant burial ground formed part of a larger cemetery in the *commune* (borough) of St Josse near Porte de Louvain. In 1877 this cemetery was closed and the land was built on. In the Brontës' time it was in countryside outside the city. Although it is now a residential area, a trace of the site remains in the form of a plot of grass in front of an apartment building in a wide street lined by mainly nineteenth-century houses. Some of the graves were relocated to the vast new cemetery in Evere on the outskirts of Brussels, but Martha and Julia's have never been found there.

I first visited the site of the St Josse cemetery on a summer evening after a thunderstorm and rain, the typical Brussels summer weather described in both *The Professor* and *Villette*; both Lucy and Crimsworth are caught in such storms, Crimsworth when accompanying Frances to her lodgings soon after his reunion with her in the Protestant cemetery. Proof that Brussels weather has not changed in the intervening century and a half was provided when Brontë Society members, assembled on 26 June 1980 for the unveiling of the plaque commemorating Charlotte and Emily, were interrupted by one of the city's violent storms.

Little along the route taken by Charlotte Brontë to the cemetery, probably a 40-minute walk from the Pensionnat, would be recognised by her today. The city gate she used to pass through, the Porte de Louvain, is no longer standing. In its place is the messy, modern and charmless Place Madou, the site of one of the city's tallest buildings. Chaussée de Louvain, along which Charlotte would have walked, is now a shopping street. However, the residential area around the site of the old cemetery, with its tall, irregular brick terraces developed after her time, looked tranquil when I first saw it in the late afternoon sunshine that succeeded the rain.

I tried to imagine Charlotte arriving here in her lonely second year in Brussels without Emily. Mary Taylor, too, had now departed to teach in Germany. Most of her other English friends had also left the city. It is still a common experience in Brussels today: you make friends, expatriates like yourself, then lose them when they move on, back to their home countries or on to a new posting abroad.

So Charlotte took solitary walks, no doubt brooding obsessively about Heger and wondering why he seemed to be trying to avoid her of late. Thinking too about her sister, her absent friends, and the friend who was dead. By her grave Charlotte would have thought of that vivacious 23-year old who was now lying there and of her family, the lively, unconventional Taylor household where she used to stay in Yorkshire and was to describe in *Shirley*.

Brussels Brontë Group members visiting the site of the old Protestant cemetery

Standing on the spot where Charlotte had stood, now not far from the European quarter, I tried to picture the country graveyard she had known. As so often in places in Brussels associated with her, I was struck afresh by the weirdness of her having been there at all. The strangeness, too, of Martha Taylor, another Yorkshire girl, ending up here, destined to stay on in the city, never to leave it, after her sister and friends had abandoned it never to return.

37. *The city cemetery in Evere*

Where was Martha now? Were she and Julia taken to Evere, and if not, what happened to them?

Eric Ruijssenaars' intention had been to investigate this, but he had not had time. We knew it was highly improbable that they had been re-buried there, but we all love playing detective and everyone likes a treasure hunt. Which is why one crisp sunny day in autumn, the season in which the two girls died, a group of Brontë enthusiasts caught a bus to the cemetery in Evere to hunt for the graves. They knew that those transferred from the Protestant cemetery could be found in three of the avenues, near the main entrance. The sunlit lanes lined with trees changing to their autumn colours looked very picturesque and everyone enjoyed themselves examining headstones, but there was no sign of the ones they sought.

One tomb that can be seen in Evere is that of the Reverend Jenkins, who died in Brussels a few years after Charlotte and Emily left and whose grave was one of those transferred from the old cemetery. Adjacent to him lies one of his two sons who were British chaplains in Brussels after him, and whose thankless task it was as teenagers to escort a reluctant Charlotte and Emily to the Sunday meals at the Jenkins home which their silence made so painful. In later years he regaled British residents of the city with stories of those mealtimes.

After this excursion, an intrepid member of the group called Renate returned to the cemetery to scrutinise headstones. Again the search was fruitless. Many of the crumbling stones were covered in moss and ivy and a lot of the inscriptions had become illegible.

This was hopeless. What she needed was a list of the graves that had been transferred to Evere. She went into the office just within the cemetery gates, a high-ceilinged, peaceful and old-fashioned place, where a lone official sat on a high stool at a much-scratched wooden counter. The wall behind him was full of pigeon-holes and shelves weighed down with heavy tomes. Despite the old-fashioned appearance of his office, however, he also had a computer register of burials. A search for Martha and Julia brought up nothing, but it was not certain from the clerk's comments whether the database included all the old graves transferred. The clerk was not sure, either, whether the remains of those whose relatives did not pay for new graves were left in St Josse or brought to a mass grave in Evere.

Renate checked the information held by the Chapelle Royale, the headquarters of the Protestant church in Brussels. They have a record of the type of funeral and grave paid for by the families of Martha and Julia. Martha had a "second class" funeral and a headstone. Poor Julia got only a "third class" funeral and no stone. The Chapelle was able to confirm that neither family paid for a burial plot in perpetuity. It is therefore extremely

Brussels city cemetery, Evere

unlikely – in Julia's case surely impossible, since she didn't even have a headstone – that either family would have paid for a new grave when the cemetery was closed, assuming they had seen the notices in British newspapers announcing the closure and explaining how to obtain ground rights in the new cemetery. But there was still no definitive proof of this, and we still did not know what happened to the remains if they were not transferred.

Over the next few months Renate made further enquiries. From now on, trying to unearth information in old documents became a new interest through which she learned much about the history of the city that had been her adopted home since leaving her native Germany many decades ago.

She enquired in the St Josse borough archives whether they had the list she sought, but the staff had no information on the old cemetery. It turned out that although, in the Brontës' time, the cemetery was in St Josse, the boundaries between boroughs have since changed and the site now comes under the jurisdiction of Schaerbeek. But the archivists there couldn't tell her about the old Protestant cemetery either. Undeterred, Renate was determined to seek further.

Soon after the excursion to ascertain whether the two girls had been transferred to Evere, I myself was transferred there. My department was moved from a building in the European district, not far from the site of the old cemetery, to a new office block in the green suburb of Evere. Sometimes my lunchtime walks took me along a wide boulevard lined with apartment blocks and past the huge city cemetery where the Jenkinses lie, and where Martha and Julia might have ended up. As I passed by the gate I would think of them all. I would also think how extraordinary it was that these people from another time should be in my thoughts. They could never have imagined that someone totally unconnected to them would be thinking of them 170 years hence in a Brussels unrecognisable to them, a city of cars and lunchtime joggers and mobile phones. They were people of no importance to me in themselves yet there they were in the ragbag of my mind, jostling with more immediate and personal concerns such as the meeting at work that afternoon and the shopping I had to do on the way home. Simply because of their link with Charlotte Brontë.

I wondered whether Renate's persistence would finally uncover the truth. In the meantime I was happy to dream that someone in our group might one day come across the grave of Martha or of Julia.

Religious order

While the Brontë fans heading for the cemetery were no doubt viewed as harmless eccentrics by the inhabitants of Evere, on another occasion two of us were taken for members of a religious order. Another lady and I opened a bank account for the group. The bank employee asked what kind of association it was. We showed him one of our flyers with George Richmond's 1850 portrait of a demure, spiritual-looking Charlotte Brontë and explained that it was an association in honour of "Les Soeurs Brontë". His response showed that far from summoning up images of Heathcliff and Cathy, moors and passion, "Brontë" meant nothing at all to him, while "sisters" suggested an order of nuns. He asked "C'est une association religieuse?"

38. *Boitsfort cemetery*

There is one Brussels cemetery with a Brontë connection that is very different from the huge city burial ground in Evere. Both are in outlying districts, but the one in Boitsfort is small and intimate. In the early twentieth century the village of Boitsfort became a green suburb of "garden city" estates and is today known for its artists and much visited in spring for its cherry blossom. The graveyard, dating from the late nineteenth century, nestles on the edge of the Forêt de Soignes, the forest enfolding the leafy suburbs of the south-east.

M. Heger was buried here in 1896 and lies with his wife and one of their daughters. I first saw his tomb on a sunny evening in late summer. Continental cemeteries can appear austere and uninviting, but this one has some of the charm of an English country churchyard. The Heger family chose well when they selected this newly-opened burial place in the green outskirts of the city.

It was shown to me by an acquaintance who knew it well; it contained a much more recent grave, that of her husband. After taking me to both spots she invited me to her house nearby where, over a cup of tea, she read out some of the poems she had written, one way in which she was dealing with her bereavement.

In the cemetery I remembered Frederika Macdonald's words about how Charlotte left behind in Brussels the "grave" of a feeling she had to bury, only to revisit it in her writings. For Charlotte, leaving Brussels and Heger and then coming to realise that there could be no more real communion with him was a kind of bereavement, and she too tried to deal with it by writing poems about her loss.

> Unloved I love, unwept I weep....
>
> My life is cold, love's fire being dead....
>
> Alas ! there are who should not love,
> I to this dreary band belong...
>
> Lonely will be my life's decline,
> Even as my youth is lonely now.

Standing by the actual tomb of Heger I thought of the way in which Charlotte Brontë revisited that "grave" of her emotions in *Villette*. Writing the closing pages after years that had seen the death of her siblings and of her hopes of emotional fulfilment, she ended her novel with bereavement and solitude. Lucy is doomed to the lonely old age Charlotte anticipated for herself. M. Paul, lost at sea, is denied not just lasting union with Lucy but even a burial place.

The Heger grave in Boitsfort cemetery

The fates that awaited their real-life counterparts were somewhat different. Two years after finishing *Villette*, Charlotte died – not unloved as she had feared, but with her husband by her side after a brief but apparently happy marriage. M. Heger, after a long life, was laid beside his wife in this tree-encircled cemetery, one of the most tranquil spots in Brussels.

39. *Discovering Brussels through the Brontës*

Charlotte Brontë's second year in Brussels was largely unhappy, and as with most people who have been lonely and miserable while abroad, her state of mind coloured her attitudes towards the city and its people.

It may therefore seem ironical that my interest in her time here led me to feel more integrated in the city, to take a keener interest in its history and to meet more of its inhabitants than I would otherwise have done, an experience I share with many other Brussels residents who have joined our group or simply read *Villette*. One reason is of course that Charlotte Brontë created something positive out of negativity by transforming it into art and enabling us to share her experience. She may have had unhappy times here but it was an unhappiness that proved tremendously important for her development and creativity.

In my own case, apart from the interest of pursuing Brontë connections in the city, setting up the Brontë group brought contacts with a variety of people and institutions. Research queries brought encounters with Brussels historians. The search for a venue brought me into contact with a Brussels university. Helping one of the city libraries to organise a conference on the Brontës took me into the office of the library's director, and being involved in organising an exhibition on the Brontës in Brussels took me into the office of the Mayor in the Town Hall. A plan for a street sculpture of Charlotte and Emily led me into a sculptor's studio.

From the start the press took an interest in our group. Our first talk was announced at a time when Jane Austen's popularity was at a peak owing to a spate of TV adaptations; the Brussels press, however, predicted a "Brontë revival". Such predictions are puzzling to those of us for whom great authors do not need reviving, but this one was fulfilled when a few years later there was an explosion of Brontë films and TV series. A radio station asked for an interview. Our event was "causing a storm" and it wanted to "get in on the act". That a talk on an English novelist's infatuation for her Belgian schoolmaster organised by a newly formed literary association could be described – albeit humorously – as creating a storm in the capital of Europe is an indication of what an endearingly small and cosy capital city it is.

When organising events I gained some insights into a city which, as a newcomer and foreigner, I knew only very superficially. The press coverage of our group showed the extent to which the language division determines the Belgian cultural scene. Each French-speaking arts centre has its Flemish counterpart; there are French and Flemish libraries, French and Flemish bookshops and French and Flemish newspapers. Even if your event is in English, the neutral lingua franca which members of both camps seem increasingly happy to use, you have to make sure it is advertised on both sides of the language divide.

Each institution in the city has a counterpart on the other side of that divide. Our venue is in a French-speaking Catholic university. I also had contacts with lecturers at a Flemish-speaking Catholic university. The two once formed part of a single institution, with courses given in both languages under the same roof. Now they are located in different parts of town. Academics and students in one language camp may not be aware of events in the other even if these are in English.

In my contacts with Belgian inhabitants of the city, I found that their view of it was coloured by the language group they belonged to. I was given rather different versions of the history of Brussels by members of the two communities, based on what sometimes seemed to be opposing sets of statistics. A French speaker claimed that the majority of the inhabitants of 1840s Brussels were French-speaking. A Flemish one asserted the exact opposite. In fairness it must be said that the exact proportion is difficult to establish, since many inhabitants of Flemish origin found it expedient to speak French for reasons of work or social mobility.

Another way in which I discovered Brussels through the Brontës was through the history of the Isabelle quarter and its demolition, in some ways a microcosm of the history of the whole city. The Pensionnat was destroyed by the *grands travaux* of Leopold II, the huge redevelopment projects of the king who colonised the Congo and wanted Brussels to be something more than a miniature Paris.

His grandiose vision turned swathes of the city into a building site for much of his reign. He has not been the only culprit, though. Brussels has a tradition of *grand travaux* that throw it into a state of permanent upheaval. Projects may be botched or abandoned when a new one comes along, and one can only wish undone some of those that have been accomplished all too thoroughly, such as the covering over of the Senne, for reasons of hygiene, which left Brussels without a river.

The demolition of the Isabelle quarter at the turn of the twentieth century lasted ten years, while the subsequent development progressed so slowly the area looked like a bomb site for decades. Photos of the quarter in the early years of the century are reminiscent of parts of the city today. Huge craters appear overnight in the most unexpected places but the work on the new developments on these sites reflects the pace at which things move in the city administration. Yet despite these continual changes, you often step from one street ravaged beyond recognition to another where time seems to have stood still and where the grass between the cobblestones in front of the sleepy old terraced houses looks as if it has been left to grow undisturbed for centuries.

Even my daily commute to work can turn my thoughts to Leopold's *grands travaux*. The Pensionnat was a victim of a construction project for a rail link and a new station in central Brussels, and in common with most

The grands travaux which flattened the Pensionnat are reminiscent of many of those in Brussels today. Rue d'Isabelle, 1910/11. Photograph of the Pensionnat taken shortly before its demolition (*Brontë Parsonage Museum*)

other commuters to the city I have for years been a victim of a rail upgrade project that involves doubling the tracks on much of the commuter railway network and modernising the city's train stations. As I pick my way around stations thrown into chaos by this project on my way to and from the office, I can only pray that it won't take as long to complete as the one to link the north and south stations and build Gare Centrale, which was first planned in the nineteenth century but did not finally open until 1952.

40. *The room in the Brussels university*

*"At last Brussels seems ready to embrace the Brontës with open arms".
From an English translation of an article in Dutch by Kristien
Hemmerechts in the literary supplement of the Belgian newspaper
De Standaard on 25 April 2008, which described the activities of the
Brussels Brontë Group*

Many of the people I met in Brussels while promoting the Brontë Group
seemed to have been placed in our way by providence. My initial
disappointment at the city's apparent lack of interest in the Brontës – for
example the failure to commemorate their stay in its streets or squares –
was often mitigated by surprised gratification that so many individuals
seemed so willing to aid and abet our enterprise. I often had an almost
supernatural sense of a favourable destiny smiling on our venture. It
seemed to be a project that had been waiting to happen, needing no more
than a gentle nudge in the right direction for it to start taking on a
momentum of its own.

An example of how our path was made easy by the kindness and
enthusiasm of certain *bruxellois* is how we found a venue for our talks. The
group had grown too big for the cosy but cramped downtown venue used
for our first talk. I was investigating various alternatives, most of them
expensive or unsuitable in some way, when the perfect room was offered
to us.

One day I left some brochures advertising the group in the pigeon-holes
of the English lecturers at a small university in central Brussels. Two of
them contacted me shortly afterwards. One of them, Jean-Louis, wrote:
"What an extraordinary coincidence! A few days before receiving your
brochure I had picked up a flyer about your group in a bookshop and only
yesterday went to look at the Brontë plaque on the Palais des Beaux-Arts."

The other, Isabelle, wrote: "Our thoughts must have crossed. Only a few
days ago I was thinking of the Brontës and of Haworth, which I visited
recently, and I am thrilled to hear that the Brontë Society has a branch in
Brussels."

Since they were both interested in the Brontës and wanted their students
to attend our talks, they suggested that we collaborate with them in
organising our events and use one of their rooms for the purpose.

As so often in Brussels, first impressions were not entirely propitious.
The university building was drab and close to a shopping mall. But the
room we were offered did not seem to belong to its surroundings. It was
light-filled, had been recently refurbished and felt instantly inviting. It was
ideal for our purposes and the staff and students gave us a warm reception.

From now on, this welcoming room was the forum for our speakers.

Stevie Davies talking to the
Brussels Brontë Group

Members listening to a speaker

Maureen Peeck (in white blouse) leads readings from *Villette*

Some were based locally, others came from Britain. The softly-spoken Welsh novelist and critic Stevie Davies cast a spell in it, musing on Emily's vision of nature and animals, the "mother world", as glimpsed in some of her essays written in Belgium. The Gaskell scholar Angus Easson, white-moustached and kindly, made the journey from his adopted city of Manchester, which was also Gaskell's adopted home. In his talk he took us on the journey to Brussels made by Mrs Gaskell herself in 1856 to collect material for her *Life of Charlotte Brontë*.

After events, group members and speakers would meet around restaurant tables or in a taverne in Grand Place for further animated discussion.

One Saturday lunchtime, during a day of talks devoted to *Wuthering Heights*, a group of us repaired to a restaurant in the ubiquitous EXKI chain for a quick snack between lectures. This popular eatery in one of the city's busiest shopping streets was teeming and the Brontëites were scattered among various tables. Wandering around tray in hand in search of a seat, I heard snatches of several different conversations. At one table the topic was Nellie Dean's reliability as a narrator, at another the question of whether any moral stance is taken in *Wuthering Heights* and at a third the relative merits of different film adaptations of the novel.

For a brief half-hour in a self-service food outlet in a bustling shopping centre, the Brontës were back in Brussels.

41. *The "Belgian Essays" and the Heger descendant*

One of the speakers at our new university venue was Sue Lonoff, translator and editor of Charlotte and Emily's "Belgian essays".

In 1983, in the Berg collection of the New York Public Library, Sue, a lecturer at Harvard, experienced the kind of thrill Brian was to know years later in a Belgian museum. She came across an unpublished Brontë work. In a catalogue she spotted the name of an essay by Charlotte Brontë she had never heard of, *Lettre d'un pauvre Peintre à un Grand Seigneur* [*Letter from a Poor Painter to a Great Lord*]. It was one of the *devoirs* Charlotte wrote in Brussels for M. Heger. How many such unpublished Belgian essays were there?

Most of the extant compositions written in French by Charlotte and Emily in Brussels ended up outside Belgium. Some are in Haworth, others in various libraries in Britain, and the rest scattered across the USA from New York to California. When Sue Lonoff came across the one that gave her the idea for her project, only half of them had been published. She decided to bring out the first collected edition, with English translations of each essay and annotations. In the pre-digital age this involved a lot of travelling to look at the manuscripts on the spot.

Her project took her to Brussels, for some of the essays did stay there, with the Heger family. M. Heger often kept copies of the compositions of his brightest pupils, so it's not surprising that his collection included some of the Brontës'. He is known to have given some away as souvenirs to fans visiting the Pensionnat, doubtless one reason why so many landed up in the USA. But four of them have remained in the possession of the Heger family to this day. The keeper of these manuscripts today is François Fierens, the great-great-great-grandson of Constantin Heger through Constantin's son Paul.

This little collection comprises three of Charlotte's essays (*The Caterpillar*, *The Fall of the Leaves* and *The Death of Moses*) and one of Emily's, a minor effort, a letter beginning *Ma chère Maman*.

Charlotte's Belgian essays are of course of interest because of Heger's influence on her approach to writing. We know from Charlotte herself that she loved reverting to being a pupil. Apart from the interest of seeing Heger's comments, transcribed in Sue Lonoff's edition, some of the themes treated by Charlotte throw light on her concept of her role as a writer – reflections on the nature of inspiration and genius, as in *The Fall of the Leaves*. Sue Lonoff points out that not all Heger's amendments to Charlotte's compositions may strike us as improvements. He made her a more disciplined craftsman and she relished the *devoirs* as a means of dialogue with him, but having absorbed what she needed from him she remained true to her own instincts and inspiration.

It is difficult to know whether Emily absorbed anything from Heger at all. We do know that initially at least she resisted his instructions to imitate great writers, and that despite her defiance he seems to have admired her intellect even more than Charlotte's. Some of Emily's Belgian essays (notably *The Butterfly*) provide insights into her philosophical ideas, as when she muses on the purpose of a world in which nature is "an inexplicable problem" since "it exists on a principle of destruction", and her treatment of the topics assigned was often more original than Charlotte's.

Emily's essays, given the lack of more personal documents relating to her time in Brussels, are also of interest as a record of her stay at the Pensionnat. Used as she was to setting her own writing agenda in the Gondal stories she wrote with Anne, she cannot always have taken kindly to writing to order on the subjects assigned to her by Heger and it is hard to imagine her being fired by the subject of *Ma chère Maman*, a letter from a homesick girl to her mother asking to be allowed to go home from boarding school. Emily, of course, had barely known her mother. But given her homesickness at the Pensionnat and the other schools where she had spent brief periods as pupil or teacher, some chords may have been struck in her as she dutifully or reluctantly wrote this little letter.

On a lighter note, Sue Lonoff referred in her talk to us to a minor French composition assignment in which Emily gets fun out of her subject, a letter from a music mistress in reply to a pupil's invitation to a musical soirée. Declining the invitation, the teacher is consoled for any disappointment by the thought that she thereby escapes the mortification of being shown up by her pupil's performance: "Forgive me if I advise you to choose a time when everyone is occupied with something other than music, for I fear that your performance will be a little too remarkable". (Emily of course took piano lessons in Brussels and was also the unpopular music teacher of some of the younger pupils at the Pensionnat).

While transcribing the *devoirs* in M. Fierens' keeping, Sue Lonoff had stayed at his house close to the site of the Pensionnat. When she returned to Brussels to talk to our group, she invited him and his wife to join group members for dinner at one of the snug old-fashioned restaurants in Grand Place. At first sight he appears to bear scant resemblance to the "little man" Charlotte described as "choleric and irritable", as he is tall and quietly-spoken and appears mild-mannered rather than irascible, but perhaps his charm and intellect are reminiscent of Constantin's.

One trait did recall Paul Emmanuel. I had heard from someone who had met him that, like M. Paul, for whom Lucy makes a watchguard, M. Fierens often wore a watch and chain. When asked to confirm this he promptly produced from his pocket the watch he took to carrying when his wristwatch was snatched by a thief in South America.

I had a real sense of him as a living link with Heger when he recounted how as a child, staying with his grandparents M. and Mme Pechère (Paul

Meeting with a Heger descendant.
From left to right, Brian Wilks, Mme Fierens, M. Fierens, Maureen Peeck,
Helen MacEwan, Sue Lonoff, Myriam Campinaire, Sue Wilks

Pechère was Constantin's great-grandson) he used to sleep in a room that was a "family temple" to the memory of Constantin and Paul Heger, and grew up knowing about Charlotte Brontë, albeit only as a minor figure in the family history.

I had the same sense of a still strong link with the past when he told us that he sang in the choir of the church where Constantin Heger worshipped – St Jacques-sur-Coudenberg in Place Royale, whose bells Charlotte heard each Sunday and Lucy refers to in *Villette*.

The following day he came to hear Sue Lonoff's talk on the Belgian essays. Just before the start of the lecture he said he had something to show us. He drew out of his briefcase the manuscripts of the essays of Charlotte and Emily's that had stayed in the Heger family, handsomely bound.

It is always thrilling to see the handwriting of a famous writer. It is exciting enough to look at Brontë manuscripts in the British Library or the Parsonage, but somehow the thrill of seeing them in a much more unlikely setting was even greater. We were in a lecture room in a twentieth-century functional institutional building surrounded by streets full of Saturday shoppers. And here was Constantin Heger's descendant casually pulling out of his case the exercise books of Charlotte and Emily, two girls who came to study in this city so far from home.

The sight of their notebooks brought home the fact that they really had been here, in Brussels. The shock of realising this anew always seemed to bring me closer to them than I had ever felt in the Parsonage.

Line of descent from M. Heger:

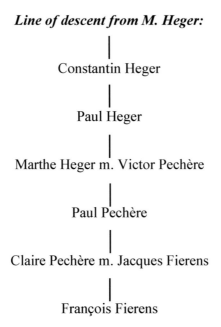

Constantin Heger

Paul Heger

Marthe Heger m. Victor Pechère

Paul Pechère

Claire Pechère m. Jacques Fierens

François Fierens

42. *Victorian banquet*

The memorable meal with the Heger descendant in Grand Place was just one of many in Brussels eaten in celebration of the Brontës.

Eating is taken almost as seriously in Belgium as in France. Amidst her negativity about so many aspects of her life in Brussels, Charlotte was enthusiastic about the food, showing a hearty appreciation of the simple but tasty fare at the Pensionnat. Probably struck by the contrast with the more monotonous diet at the Parsonage, in *Villette* she describes with relish the simplest things on the school menu, such as the breakfast *pistolets* (rolls) and *brioches*, even waxing enthusiastic about *tartines* (slices of bread and butter).

In a capital that enjoys eating so much, it is not surprising that food has played its role in our group events. When a Brussels library organised a day of talks on "The Brontës in Brussels" it included a lecture on Victorian food. The lecturer, from the *Centre de Gastronomie Historique*, which provides courses on the history of food and devises historical banquets, did his research thoroughly. His was the last of six lectures in what turned into a literary marathon – Belgian events, like Belgian meals, not being known for their brevity. By the time our gastronomic speaker's turn came, we were flagging; hungry as well as tired.

It's a pity our attention kept wandering to the prospect of actual food and drink, since the talk was packed with information. We listened to a comparison of English and Belgian food in the 1840s, were guided through some of the pages of Mrs Beeton and instructed on the order in which dishes were served.

All this information was about to be put to practical use. This lecture, like all the others, was in reality just a prelude to the event everyone was looking forward to with most relish. Like any organisers of any event in Belgium, the conference organisers had seized eagerly on an excuse to hold a meal. A conference on the Brontës in Brussels? Why not get a scholar to hold forth about Victorian food and then all go off and have a Victorian banquet?

So at the close of the gastronomic talk we were released only briefly, to convene again in a restaurant in the Grand Place area, an old-fashioned establishment that had been used by our group in the past. With its dark panelling, rich, heavy furnishings and ponderous elderly waiters, it had a Dickensian feel well suited to lovers of things Victorian. After one of our dinners here we had had readings from *Villette*, the staff looking on impassively at our odd proceedings.

Our own repasts had been modest affairs. Today's dinner was on a much grander scale and was principally for the regular habitués of the library's

116

MENU

FIRST COURSE

Oxtail soup removed by Boiled Turbot with Lobster Sauce
Garnished with Fried Smelts and Whitings

ENTRÉES

Lamb Cutlets and Peas
Oyster Patties
Fricandeau of Veal

SECOND COURSE

Tête de Veau en Tortue
Roast Lamb and Mint Sauce
Asparagus Pudding
Vegetables (Sea-Kale, Broccoli & Spinach) and Fresh Salad

THIRD COURSE

Duckling Removed by Cabinet Pudding and Syllabub
Lemon jelly
Trifles
Apple Cheesecakes
Rhubarb tart

DESSERT & ICES

Victorian banquet menu

literary events, who, being Belgian, turned out en masse at the prospect of a banquet, albeit an English one.

The formality and slow-moving pace of the occasion, with a high table for VIPs, was something I had experienced at other Belgian events and it was certainly suited to a Victorian dinner. Of course Belgians are used to meals on a gargantuan scale. Writing about a stay in Brussels while touring Europe, Lewis Carroll said of a meal there: "The dinner was 'très simple', and therefore consisting of only seven courses."* At our own banquet there were fifteen dishes. But we were not allowed to make a start on them until the gastronomic expert had given us a second (somewhat briefer) talk to explain some points of Victorian table etiquette he had not had time to cover that afternoon. Belgians are nothing if not thorough in their approach to food.

It is not every day that one has the opportunity of attending an English nineteenth-century banquet served by a continental chef. This one was certainly up to the task, miraculously producing the fifteen dishes for fifty people practically single-handed. Turbot with lobster sauce, oyster patties, cabinet pudding with syllabub and custard…impossible to do justice to it all. But for the *Centre de Gastronomie Historique*, creating fifteen-course gala dinners is all in a day's work.

One person present did not wholly enjoy the experience. Eric Ruijs-senaars is a vegetarian, and in Victorian times vegetarians cannot have had an easy time. Dish after dish was brought out and he was still hungry. And the meal seemed to be interminable. He sat uneasily through the oxtail soup, lamb cutlets and fricandeau of veal. Perhaps it was the sight of the *tête de veau en tortue* that finally frayed his nerves to snapping point. Muttering excuses, he got up and made his escape.

In complete contrast to the scene of our Victorian meal is a modern museum restaurant in Place Royale, in the building which in the Brontës' time was the Hôtel Bellevue where Wellington stayed, close to the intersection of Rue Terarken and Rue d'Isabelle. Here group members convene for informal lunches, and literary talk often continues well into the afternoon. The restaurant is a stone's throw from the Pensionnat site. It's pleasant to think that the Brontës are the magnet that draws us all together to eat on this spot so close to the place where, in 1842, Charlotte and Emily enjoyed their *brioches*.

43. *The Dutch singer and the Celtic connection*

*The Brontë group often brought me into contact with people who were
inspired creatively by the Brontës – Marina with her calligraphy,
Selina with her illustrations. Among these were a musician,
an artist and a novelist.*

When I met the Dutch musician Veronica Metz, she had just recorded an
album of musical settings of some of Emily's poems. She had come to
Brussels to sing them for us and told us the story of how they came to be
written.

In 2004 Veronica visited the Parsonage museum and remembered her
father telling her about the Brontë family when she was a child. He was a
great admirer of *Wuthering Heights*. Up to her visit to Haworth she had
only known Emily as a novelist, but in the Parsonage bookshop she picked
up a book of her poems.

Some years earlier Veronica had started up a Celtic music band called
Anois in her native Netherlands. She was the band's lead singer and also
composed many of its songs. For the past seven years she had been
immersed in the world of Tolkien, setting to music the poems in *Lord of the
Rings*. The band members dressed in richly-coloured flowing robes and
sang about elves. Tolkien's universe appealed strongly to her, his vision of
a time when "the world was young, the mountains green".

Shortly before her visit to Yorkshire she had finished the Tolkien project
and was consciously or unconsciously looking for inspiration for her next
one when she lighted on Emily Brontë's poems in the bookshop on the edge
of Haworth moor. She found her inspiration as soon as she opened the

Veronica

119

book. For her the poems were magical and gave her a sense of purity and profundity. They spoke of nature, of an ethereal world beyond. Before she left Yorkshire she knew she wanted to set some of them to music for her band.

Surfing the web for information on the Brontës, she saw that there was a course on their works in the department for continuing education at the University of Utrecht, her home town. She enrolled for it. The lecturer was Maureen Peeck O'Toole, who not long afterwards was to be one of the people involved in setting up the Brussels Brontë Group.

Emily's verse was more profound, harder to understand than Tolkien's. But it had in common with Tolkien's world a mystical atmosphere that suited the band's Irish sound, incorporating harp and violin and Veronica's high, pure, angelic voice. She was excited to learn about Emily's Celtic connections, her Irish father and Cornish mother. She liked to imagine that these must somehow have spoken to her in Emily's verse.

Cover of Anois' Brontë album

In the poems selected by her, the moon shines clear from the midnight sky, stars gaze serenely from heaven into the speaker's eyes like the eyes of lovers, the house is silent, and the snow lies thick outside. Veronica's Emily is the Emily of "stars and dreams and gentle night".

Synergies

Through our group Veronica met Marina, whose calligraphy had been similarly inspired both by Celtic culture and Emily Brontë. Marina too was a fan of Ireland. On her annual holidays there she found the peace that allowed her calligraphic ideas to flow freely. Back home in Flanders, she would listen to Irish music to recreate the atmosphere of the country while working with her coloured inks. She found in Veronica's musical settings an ideal background and inspiration for her own work. In turn, Veronica commissioned her designs for album covers. They had responded to the poems for similar reasons. Once, embarking on a new design, Marina found that by coincidence or telepathy Veronica had just begun to set the same poem to music. Their collaboration was just one instance of synergies between two creative group members.

44. *A visit to an artist's studio*

At Veronica's concert I met Franklin, an artist who told me he had produced a series of works inspired by the Brontës' lives and works. He invited me to visit his studio to view them and a few days later I took up the invitation; having just heard Veronica's musical interpretations of Brontë writings I was interested in seeing Franklin's visual ones. But I often fail to appreciate modern art works and went not with any great expectations but out of curiosity.

The studio was in one of the tall narrow terraced houses lining one of Brussels' long *chaussées*. Charlotte Brontë often mentions the *chaussées* of Brussels – the main roads leading from the city, for example to Leuven in the east and Waterloo in the south, along which she tramped on solitary walks in the country and which she describes as being miry in winter and dusty in summer. It was a dusty summer's day when I went to Franklin's studio. There is something depressingly monotonous about these *chaussées*, which stretch seemingly endlessly into the flat countryside surrounding the capital. Looking around as I rang the bell, I wondered what I was about to discover in the house in the nondescript terrace in front of me.

Franklin led me up rickety stairs to a dwelling as small as Frances Henri's in *The Professor*. Books about the Brontës were piled high, all acquired in second-hand bookshops in his adopted city. Although I later found he was not without some twenty-first century gadgetry – a computer, a mobile phone – my first impression of an artist living in a garret in true nineteenth-century Romantic style was never totally effaced.

Looking at his collection of Brontë books, I asked if he had ever been to Haworth. It turned out that though his interest in the family went back years, he had never even been to England. His mental images of the place that haunted him came from the books lying around us and from pictures.

He led me up another narrow flight of stairs to his studio. Expecting it to be flooded with light on this summer's afternoon and filled with modern artwork, I found myself instead in the small darkened room – a tinkle of Bach adding to the atmosphere, the walls crammed with small pictures – that he called his "temple". Currently a temple to the Brontës. The works he wanted to show me turned out to be not paintings but drawings. Extraordinary drawings. Many of those crowding the walls measured no more than ten by fifteen centimetres. He showed me some of the tiniest first, done on the pages of a small drawing pad, some in pencil, some in ink. Executed on a scale almost as miniscule as the Brontës' juvenile manuscripts, they needed a magnifying glass to be appreciated in detail. He told me that even a small drawing often took him weeks to do, usually working through the night, while bigger ones could take months.

The pictures were full of symbolism suggested by the Brontës' works or lives but also arising naturally from the romantic world which, by temperament, Franklin inhabited. Water – a river was the river of life, a lake the Elderno Lake of one of Emily's poems –, female figures, and the moon – representing eternity – appeared again and again. In one tiny drawing, "Homage to Emily Brontë", a Lady stood by Emily's tombstone, inviting viewers to read the inscription on the stone. He explained that her beckoning hand had six fingers to represent the six Brontë children and that she was an apparition that lasted only while the moon was full. By Emily's tomb was a bird, and Keeper howling with grief for the loss of his mistress, both representing her love of animals. Emily's face could be seen looking out from one of the Parsonage windows towards the churchyard. But in the distance was also "the Hall of Eternity. Emily is there", Franklin explained. Also in the distant moors were Wuthering Heights and Cathy and Heathcliff wandering hand in hand.

The themes of death and eternity recurred constantly in his work, with death, that modern taboo, always present but always coupled with eternity and the hope of reunion with loved ones. So while tombstones made a frequent appearance, a tower on the windswept moors would symbolise "the hall of eternity".

On the backs of the drawings, lines were inscribed in tiny script:

> Once drinking deep of that divinest anguish, How could I seek the empty world again?

> A dark evening, threatening thunder....

Franklin's love of symbols extended to his own speech and he used metaphor and personification as naturally as any nineteenth-century poet. I soon found that he was liable to speak of his devotion to Lady Art, or observe that he had "spent the night in Lady Fantasy's arms". I found it hard to imagine a modern-day artist from my own country describing a night working on a picture in such terms!

The high point of this private viewing was when Franklin produced two bigger drawings, "Jane Eyre" and "Gondal". Despite their size, every inch was richly-textured, packed with closely-worked detail. "Jane Eyre" had taken him eight months, "Gondal" six. In the former, Thornfield Hall looms dark against a background of stormy sky, branches of trees tossed by the wind, a full moon. In a description of the picture for an exhibition Franklin has written: "The trees seem to move, like Tolkien's 'ents', the whole picture is in agitation showing in its motion the turbulent and agitated world of the Brontës' books". The tiny figure of Jane is silhouetted in the doorway of the Hall. In a corner is a little church, the scene of the aborted wedding.

The most peculiar work of all was "Gondal", a large drawing but again,

Detail of "Gondal" (the original drawing measures approximately 20 x 30 cm)

covered with a mass of detail that at a distance simply looks like a texture built up of repeated abstract designs but close up turns out to be a host of little figures that produce the kind of giddiness induced by Richard Dadd's scenes of elfland.

Franklin describes it thus: "The many tiny figures and faces are drawn from Yorkshire lore. The Brontë children would listen to these stories from the mouth of Tabby, so these creatures are goblins, boggards, fairies, demons, elemental beings, ghost dogs, and you can also see fairy-haunted dells, passages, and stones and gemstones, doors where you hear a knock or a cry but you find no-one behind, only it does not frighten you, for you look with the eyes of innocence so no harm will come to you, an enchanted fairy bed." In the darkened room I was surrounded by the visions of an unusual mind.

In the drawing room at Thornfield Hall, Jane shows Rochester her drawings of female figures amid livid skies and stormy moonlit seas. Rochester gazes at her pictures for a long time, transfixed. They are "strange", he says. (From her descriptions they do indeed seem a far cry from the landscapes and portraits to be found on the average Victorian young lady's easel). "The thoughts...are elfish. These eyes in the Evening Star you must have seen in a dream. What meaning is that in their depth? And who taught you to paint wind?"

In Franklin I found two qualities common in creative people: intensity and childlikeness. Like children, artists live in the world of their imagination undistracted by the "real" one and they continue to see things with a child's intensity. The Romantics had these qualities more than most. The Brontës remained in the world of Gondal and Angria long into adulthood.

An hour later, after a cup of exotic-tasting tea, I emerged from the darkened studio into the *chaussée*. The Brussels sky was now overcast, yet the light seemed dazzling compared with the gloom of Franklin's abode. I stood blinking and disorientated. People were going by talking on mobile phones. I was in the twenty-first century again. Franklin's evocations of the Brontës' imaginative world had plunged me into a place where time did not exist. What he expressed with images such as the moon shining serene in turbulent skies could be referred to only through words almost never used in the hurried world of today, concerned only with the present. Words such as "eternity".

45. *Franklin goes to Haworth*

Franklin's dream was to exhibit his work in the place where he himself had never been, but which was often present in his imagination. He called it "a place I cherish at a distance." When I offered to take copies of his work to Haworth and show them to the director of the Parsonage Museum he was almost as moved at the thought of his artwork being in Haworth as if he had been making the trip there himself.

The director looked at Franklin's drawings as attentively as Rochester does at Jane's. He said they were interested in the idea of an exhibition. A few months later Franklin, with the original drawings under his arm to show the museum staff, scraped together the money for the fare and made his way to Haworth. In e-mails, in the weeks before he left he had looked forward excitedly to this first trip to England.

"Haworth! Finally! Is it possible? Am I dreaming? Is it true? I'm really going to Brontëland.... The moors call to me.... Wuthering Heights is waiting there for me...."

But on his return, when I asked him for his impressions, he did not seem able to report them in conventional mode. What he felt could only be fully expressed in drawings, though he did attempt to write down his sensations on crossing the threshold of the Parsonage in impressionistic prose poems:

"I am stepping into a world which I believe is still inhabited by one of the hands of God, God's true nature, Art, therefore this house is still alive.... How many hours of study, solitude spent in these rooms? The clock.... beats its rhythm to the pace of poems and novels word for word, the clock is never silent; it is the heart of the house echoing in time in distant footsteps and voices approaching and fading away as real as your own, the coming and going of people from room to room or the late afternoon shadows moving about unknown to the human eye, kitchen sounds of cutlery and pans....insistent and talkative wind wooing and knocking on windows in long-lost articulations...."

He would have loved to be able to stay longer in Haworth, working on new art projects. But one ambition had been realised. The museum people had invited him to exhibit his drawings at the Parsonage.

46. *The novelist*

Another Brontë enthusiast who made the trip to Haworth around this time was Jolien Janzing, a journalist and novelist, of Dutch parentage but brought up in Belgium. She wrote an article for a magazine about her visit. Her lively impressions were like those of any other first-time visitor; it's hard to find something to say that hasn't been said by previous literary pilgrims. She spoke to the museum director about what it was that kept the tourists pouring through the Parsonage door. She noted the number of recent books on the Brontës in the bookcase in his office and in the shops on Main Street where she made acquisitions for her own growing collection.

On her return from the moors and the steep streets of Haworth, back in the flat landscape of Flanders where she had grown up, Jolien wrote her article, but her journey to that very different landscape of the Brontës' childhood had a more long-term purpose, since she had just started working on a much more ambitious and personal project.

In Haworth she had noted the proliferation of books spawned by the Brontës' lives and works. There seemed to be no end to the re-telling of their life stories or re-working of their fiction. But what about Charlotte and Emily's time in Brussels? None of the books she had browsed through in the village shops had been interested primarily in that.

When I first met Jolien soon after her visit to Yorkshire she was excited about the project she had embarked on: a novel about the Brontës' stay in Brussels. With a couple of books already behind her, she was ambitious about her writing career and eager to start on the next one. She knew that she wanted it to be an historical novel about a real person, but searched for some time for a subject before hitting on the Brontës when she discovered that they had lived in Brussels. Although she had read *Villette* as a teenager she had not realised this and she knew that the Brontës' link with Brussels would be new for many of her readers, who were both Flemish and Dutch.

Jolien was ebullient about her discovery. She could hardly believe her luck in stumbling on it. The Brontës had been in Brussels and she'd never known it until now, just when she was looking for a theme for her book! The subject that had thus fallen into her lap, a little-known fact about such well-known figures, was ideal for her. She had always liked the Brontës since her mother introduced her to *Jane Eyre* at the age of ten. And she was living in Belgium, able to do the Brussels research needed for her book, provide a Belgian take on the Brontës' Brussels adventure.

The most amazing part of it all was that, as far as she and I knew, no-one before her had attempted exactly the same thing – a novel dealing exclusively with Charlotte and Emily's time in Brussels.

Her Dutch publisher liked the idea of a novel set in Brussels, a city that appealed to readers in the Netherlands – close to them but slightly exotic at

Jolien

the same time. Jolien wanted to fill in the background to the Brontës' life there by exploring the history, everyday life and politics of the city at that period.

She told me she had empathised with Charlotte ever since her early identification with Jane Eyre, who at the start of the book is the same age as Jolien when she first read it. Looking at her, I felt slightly sceptical about this claim. What could she have in common with Charlotte and her "plain", physically "insignificant" and "invisible" heroines? One point in common was the sense of being an outsider, she said: as a Dutch person growing up in Belgium she had shared this feeling with Charlotte. Another thing she shared was her drive and ambition, the wish to prove herself through writing.

She was naturally interested too in exploring the character of Constantin Heger. Her own experience as the daughter of a Catholic father and Protestant mother, brought up as a Protestant in a Catholic country – at school she was given religious instruction apart from the rest of her classmates, rather as Charlotte and Emily were excused from religious observance at the Pensionnat – gave her insights into differences between the two religions that she thought explained some aspects of Heger's personality and behaviour. The flirtatious element in his teaching style, while never overstepping certain limits, perhaps reflected a more relaxed attitude typical of a Catholic culture that would have been novel to Charlotte, reared in Protestantism with its different cultural mores.

One element not found in previous books about the Brontës was a sub-plot Jolien was introducing about King Leopold I's young mistress, Arcadie Claret, by whom he had two children. Arcadie was the mistress of a married man; Charlotte had intense feelings about a married man. Arcadie appeared to be a woman who had everything while Charlotte was deeply unsatisfied with her own life.

In Jolien I found something I encountered in many other Brontë enthusiasts I met in Brussels: a freshness, the excitement of a discovery, the sense that the Brontës' stay in Brussels gives those of us who live here a special, secret link with them that no-one else shares. It makes them "ours" – "our" Brontës – just as for Yorkshire people the Brontës of Haworth are "their" Brontës.

47. *Martha and Julia (III)*

Amid all the events, developments and projects taking place in our group, no definitive progress had been made in Renate's quest to find out what happened to the remains of Martha Taylor and Julia Wheelwright when the old Protestant cemetery was closed. I did not altogether regret this lack of information. Further investigation might simply confirm the impossibility of locating them, and it was more exciting to leave the question unanswered for the time being and make occasional further forays to Evere cemetery to peer at the names on the old nineteenth-century tombs there.

To some cool outsiders this quest may have seemed mad: not just hopeless but pointless. There was no indication that anyone in the Taylor family saw fit to pay for a new grave for Martha when the old one was dug up, although her sister Mary was still living and the closure was announced in The Times. No-one seems to have cared much about her remains back then. No-one today would ever have heard of her had she not been the sister of Charlotte Brontë's friend.

Yet there were people living in the twenty-first century who were interested enough to search for her, and not just Brontë enthusiasts in Brussels. A Spanish Brontë Society member wrote that she was doing a dissertation on Charlotte Brontë and had just spent a weekend in the city. She had read on our blog about the search for the graves and was intrigued enough to want to look for them herself. Aptly enough, her visit was over the weekend of Halloween and All Saints' Day, a time of year when Belgians pay visits to family graves. Paloma's visit was of a more unusual kind, yet her enquiry must have had a familiar ring to the clerk among his records in the quiet office by the cemetery gates in Evere, who had already been visited by at least one member of our group. Although he informed her politely that the name of Martha Taylor was not to be found on his computer, she strolled hopefully around the leaf-strewn avenues peering at inscriptions before catching her plane back to Madrid at the airport up the road.

Despite the charm in the uncertainty surrounding the grave, Renate still wanted to find some definitive proof that it was not in Evere – for she had little hope that it was. She had been an efficient handler and filer of information in her working life and wanted to be able to "close the file" on this case. Surely, somewhere in an archive in Brussels was that list she was seeking, of graves transferred from the old cemetery. If Martha's name was not in it she could shelve this bit of Brontë research once and for all.

Her enquiries, however, received rather vague and contradictory answers. One official was of the opinion that such a list had never existed, another that it had existed but was now lost, another was sure that there must be such a list – in someone else's archives! In one office it was suggested that it might be in a box in the basement with other records that no-one had got round to sorting.

In the City Archives in the converted warehouse near Gare du Midi so beloved of Eric Ruijssenaars, Derek Blyth and Brian Bracken, just such a box was brought out for her, full of old papers concerning the clearance of the old cemetery. Here she did come across something relevant to her quest, some instructions to the effect that remains not given individual graves in the new cemetery were to be interred in a section in the east of it. From this document it is possible to locate that section today. Now at least she knew the spot where the two girls almost certainly ended up.

Meanwhile, she had obtained a book about Brussels cemeteries which gave details of some of the most important British graves transferred to Evere from the Protestant burial ground. Among the administrative offices at whose doors she had knocked in vain was the city department responsible for death certificates and burials. Wearying by now of the search, she thought she would return there to make one last attempt. She took the book with her.

She knew that this department had computerised records of burials. A previous search for Martha's name had drawn a blank but what Renate wanted to verify was whether the names of *all* those transferred had been entered in this computer database. She showed the official in charge the names listed in her book and he searched for some of them in his database.

And this proved to be the breakthrough, Renate's eureka moment. When names of people actually transferred were entered in the system – and only then – it became apparent that this register of burials did in fact contain records of all those taken from St Josse for re-burial in individual graves in Evere.

Martha and Julia were not among them. In that sense, the outcome of Renate's search had been disappointing, but here at last was the proof she had been seeking that they had not been among those given new graves.

The information she had been searching for had been computerised all along. A further absurd twist was added to the story when this helpful official hinted that the paper registers from which the information had been obtained were likely to be in the place where her search had begun: at the Evere cemetery.

It was perhaps understandable that not all the people she had approached had been so willing to devote time to a query which must have seemed hardly worth pursuing, since given that the Taylor and Wheelwright families did not originally pay for a grave in perpetuity, the likelihood that they did so in the 1880s was practically non-existent.

Her consolation for the frustrations she had experienced was that if the proof she had been seeking had come to light on the first day of her enquiries, she would have had a much less interesting time – like Helen Cooper, the *Villette* editor who was hampered by lack of information in her

Renate

search for the site of the Pensionnat but enjoyed the challenge of hunting it down.

She decided to "close the file on the case". As a symbolic act of closure, she paid a last visit to Evere cemetery and located the site of the mass grave. I wondered whether she was the first mourner for the two girls in the spot where we now had reason to believe they were taken.

In *Shirley*, Charlotte writes hauntingly of the graveyard in an unspecified foreign country where Jessie Yorke – who teased, charmed and fascinated everyone she encountered – was left to sleep forever alone among the willows and cypresses. But Martha was not to be allowed to sleep on undisturbed in the picturesque graveyard Charlotte knew.

For those who "believe in ghosts" it's difficult to know which part of Brussels Martha and Julia's would choose to haunt today. It is hard to imagine them among the apartment blocks of Evere. Would they not prefer to pay occasional ghostly visits to the quiet site of the old cemetery, albeit now surrounded by Brussels town houses, where they were first laid to rest?

Whatever our views on "ghosts", our interest in the dead gives them a life after death, since they live on in our minds. In return, they give us a feeling of intimacy with them. We often feel so much closer to them than to the living, the people we see around us every day but of whose thoughts and feelings we know little or nothing. Because we know so much about Charlotte Brontë, those whose paths crossed hers live with her in our imagination. Even Martha Taylor, a minor player in Charlotte's story but a vital figure in her own right. As we walked in the Brontës' footsteps in the city where she died, it was this posthumous life of Martha's in our minds that gave zest to our ultimately fruitless search for her grave.

48. *Searchers*

Through the Brontës I met many immigrants in the city who had come in search of a new life. But in fact everyone I met through the group was engaged in a quest because of their interest in a long-dead family.

For enthusiasts of all kinds, life is a quest. Literary enthusiasts re-read their favourite novels in search of the things they missed the last time. They listen to yet another talk on a favourite writer or read yet another biography in the hope of coming across fresh nuggets of information. Seeking more knowledge of the writers they love, the people those writers knew and the places they visited, they are drawn on in an ever-widening, ever-deepening circle of interest. The more they learn the more they want to learn.

Our search for the graves of Martha Taylor and Julia Wheelwright in Brussels cemeteries can be explained only in terms of this interest in anything and everything to do with a writer whose life and books become an important part of our imagination. I want to end this book, however, not with the search for the two dead friends of Charlotte Brontë but with one man's search for Charlotte Brontë herself.

49. *In Grand Place*

It was an afternoon in December and we had gathered for a Christmas celebration in a room at a taverne in Grand Place, the kind of gathering I had dreamed of years before in the Old White Lion in Haworth.

We had just watched some members performing the playlet *Christmas Dinner at Haworth Parsonage*, a humorous sketch published in Punch in the 1930s.* The occasion as imagined by the playwright is not a festive one. The family are morose and moody – until Branwell rolls in the worse for drink, when things liven up but in the wrong way – with Charlotte the gloomiest of the lot; the explanation, "She broods on Brussels", which prompts Patrick to ask for the sprouts, had earned a laugh from the audience. Was it the first time these lines had been heard in Brussels?

Now, the entertainment over, people were talking in pairs and small groups. In one of these was Elle, on a rare visit to Brussels, her auburn hair a warm blaze of colour in a corner. Derek was telling Maureen and Selina about one of his long-cherished projects: to organise a concert in the Park based on the one Lucy hears on the night of the fête. Eric and Brian were as deep in conversation about things discovered in Brussels archives as they were frequently deep in the archives themselves.

Grand Place in 1843
(*Royal Library of Belgium*)

Dusk was deepening in the fairytale square through the mullioned windows as I fell into conversation with a member of the group I had never spoken to before, a young man called Carlo. I asked him how he had first become attracted by the Brontës and which of them interested him most.

"Charlotte has always been the one who interests me. I don't feel I *know* Emily or Anne. Charlotte I feel I know better than anyone else in the world."

Carlo was slight and delicate-looking with rather a melancholy expression in his eyes. I felt at once that what he had to say about Charlotte Brontë would be something a little out of the ordinary.

"Tell me about it," I said. I had mentioned that I was writing a book about the people I had met in Brussels through the Brontës, and he had said he had no objection to telling me his own Brontë story.

"How long have you got?" he asked.

"As long as it takes."

"It might take some time. It's not easy to explain, and I'll have to tell you something about my life to show you why Charlotte has been so important in it. Actually I've never told anyone the whole story of what I feel about Charlotte because they would just think I'm crazy. Today is the first time I've been with a whole group of people who are interested in the Brontës and I think people like you may understand."

It sounded as if I was about to hear the kind of revelation I had so enjoyed on my first stay in Haworth.

Filling me in on the background to his first encounter with Charlotte Brontë did take some time. He explained that since birth he had been dogged by health problems that had prevented him from having a fully normal childhood or adolescence and, at one stage in his teenage years, led him to shun the company of his peers, with whom he always felt at a physical disadvantage, and turn to novels instead. All this reading made him very romantic and he was always in love with some girl around whom he wove dramas and mysteries. His ideal woman sounded to me like the typically "feminine" heroine of Victorian novels: beautiful of course, sensitive, refined.

Then when he was sixteen and in the depths of adolescent depression about what he perceived as his social inadequacy – the only girls he had so far approached romantically had been the ones in his fantasies – he read *Jane Eyre*.

Nothing was ever the same again. The novel brought about an instant and tremendous change in his perception of women. It gave him inside knowledge of a woman's whole personality and soul for the first time. This woman, Jane Eyre, didn't just have the "feminine" virtues he had hitherto admired. She was as strong in character as a man, as intelligent, self-aware, passionate. She was in fact everything that, in his innermost self, despite his frustrations, he felt himself to be. He felt, to cite Rochester's words to Jane, "My equal is here, and my likeness."

"I think Charlotte had a kind of androgynous spirit, equal parts feminine and masculine – perhaps that's why she was accused by critics of being "unfeminine" – and I believe I am divided in the same way.

"Reading this particular book was a different experience to any other. It was as if everything I had read up to then had been slightly blurred. With Charlotte Brontë's writing, everything was in focus, clearer and sharper. She seemed to touch every part of my soul and rouse every energy inside me. Reading *Jane Eyre*, I felt that I was really living to the full as I never had before. It was an awakening, an initiation, like being raised from the dead.

"But that wasn't all. Reading Charlotte Brontë I became aware of myself for the first time, and I felt that I was exactly the same as her. Her soul matched mine. I recognised myself in her. Helen, I *am* Charlotte!"

For a moment I was not Helen but Nellie, Nellie Dean listening to Cathy talking about Heathcliff. But Cathy was a character in a book. Did real people ever feel such total identification with another human being?

Carlo's story was the most extreme account of identification with one of the Brontës I had heard. Was what he felt something really unusual or had he just been one of the countless sensitive teenagers for whom an encounter with the mind of a particular author is a turning point, a means of defining themselves?

He told me how he empathised in particular with one thing he sensed in Charlotte: a feeling of physical inferiority, of lost opportunities. Like her, he knew what it was to be at a party and not be able to enjoy it, to sit in a corner and analyse everyone in the room as a form of compensation for all the things not within his reach.

But this identification with Charlotte wasn't the whole story. After reading *Jane Eyre* he also had a clear idea of the kind of woman he wanted to find. In her portrayal of Rochester, Charlotte describes exactly what she was looking for in a man. He is in fact someone with all her own characteristics. Until *Jane Eyre*, Carlo had only a vague idea of the person he was looking for. Now he knew that it must be someone with Charlotte's essential qualities.

There was no need to ask him whether his search so far had been successful.

"I know it's not going to be easy to find her. Maybe you're thinking, impossible. What if that perfect partner does exist somewhere but I never meet her or she doesn't wait for me, chooses somebody else? But I have to hope that somewhere there is someone waiting and searching for me – someone like Charlotte."

Did Charlotte Brontë ever entertain any hope of finding a real-life Rochester? When she created Rochester, had she already seen in Heger the twin soul she knew she could never be united with? In her year of marriage with Arthur Bell Nicholls did she, to her own surprise, find genuine happiness with someone so different from the teacher she had idolised or the hero she had invented as his surrogate? What would the outcome of Carlo's own quest be?

By this time there were only a few other people left, talking quietly. I looked round the room. At one point in our conversation I had fancied for a moment that I had glimpsed, out of the corner of my eye, a guest I had not noticed earlier. She was sitting alone watching and listening in a shadowy corner not far from us. I recognised her – a small figure in grey. She looked as if she had been tramping the streets of Brussels and was glad to be out of the cold. But the next moment she had vanished. I must have imagined her.

As Carlo finished his story I thought of all the others I had heard in Brussels, all the people I had met. Why had I met them and heard their stories in *Brussels*? Because the Brontës had been here. It was because Charlotte Brontë had been in Brussels that I started the group thanks to which Carlo's path and mine had crossed. Reading *Villette* in Brussels had created a strong link for me with Charlotte. "*She* was *here*. And now *I'm* here." And that in turn created links with people like Carlo from different cultures. Here we were, two foreigners in Brussels, just as Charlotte had been. Talking about her.

Night was falling fast. By now Grand Place was lit up in all its glory. I gazed out of the window and thought how my Brontë encounters had illuminated Brussels for me.

Everyone else had departed and now Carlo, too, took his leave and went out into the twilight. I watched from the window as he crossed the square and turned down a side street. As I left the room I looked around and thought of all those who had been gathered there, talking about projects and experiences. And as I walked through the streets of Brussels I thought about the little figure in grey.

Notes

Abbreviation: PL = Ruijssenaars, Eric, *Charlotte Brontë's Promised Land.*

1. *Along Rue de la Loi*
p. 5 Thackeray, William Makepeace, "Little Travels and Roadside Sketches". *Fraser's Magazine*, May 1844.

3. *Down the Belliard steps*
p. 18 Cumberland, Gerald, "Charlotte Brontë's street in Brussels today". *Cornhill Magazine*, 1911. Reprinted in *PL*, pp. 84-86.

4. *Pilgrims to the Pensionnat*
p. 20 Trafton, Adeline, "A Visit to Charlotte Brontë's School at Brussels". *Scribner's Monthly*, 3:2, December 1871. Reprinted in PL, pp.. 58-60.

p. 20 Cumberland, Gerald, Charlotte Brontë's street in Brussels today. *Cornhill Magazine*, 1911. Reprinted in *PL*, pp. 84-86.

p. 20 Brontë, Charlotte, *The Professor*, Chapter 7, has a passage beginning: "Belgium! name unromantic, unpoetic....". Charlotte, or Crimsworth, nevertheless goes on to say that it is a name "that whenever uttered has in my ear a sound, in my heart an echo, such as no other assemblage of syllables, however sweet or classic, can produce."

p. 21 Spielmann, M.H., "Charlotte Brontë in Brussels". *The Times Literary Supplement*, 1916. Reprinted in *PL*, pp. 93-101.

p. 21 MacDonald, Frederika, *The Secret of Charlotte Brontë*. London, 1914, p. 9.

5. *Eric*
p. 24 Charlotte Cory, "Heroes and Villains". *Independent Magazine*, 29 May 1993.

10. *Marina*
p. 33 "Labassecour" (farmyard/poultry-yard) was Charlotte's name for Belgium in *Villette*; "les Labassecouriens" were the Belgians.

p. 34 Hemmerechts, Kristien, article in the literary supplement of the Belgian newspaper *De Standaard*, 25 April 2008 (cited in an English translation).

15. *Research*
p. 44 *Revue Trimestrielle*, 1854, Vol. 2 pp. 279-283.

p. 45 The Spielmann citations in this chapter are taken from Spielmann, M.H., *The Inner History of the Brontë-Heger letters*. London, 1919.

17. *Researchers past and present*
p. 49 *PL*, pp. 35-37.

p. 49 De Knevett, Edgar. Letter cited in Eric Ruijssenaars, *The Pensionnat Revisited*, 2003, p. 28.

21. *The website*
p. 63 Brontë, Charlotte, "Prefatory Note to Selections from poems by Ellis Bell." In Smith, Margaret, ed., *The Letters of Charlotte Brontë*. Volume II. Clarendon Press, Oxford, 2000, p. 753.

23. *Torrent of Passion*
p. 68 Spielmann, M.H., *The Inner History of the Brontë-Heger letters*. London, 1919.

35. *Martha and Julia (II)*
p. 97 Smith, Margaret, ed., *The Letters of Charlotte Brontë*. Volume I, 1829-1847. Clarendon Press, Oxford, 1995, pp.. 280-282.

42. *Victorian Banquet*
p. 118 Carroll, Lewis, "Journal of a Tour in Russia in 1867", in *The Works of Lewis Carroll*. London, 1965, p. 968.

49. *In Grand Place*
p. 134 "Christmas Dinner at Haworth Parsonage", *Punch*, 25 December 1935. Reproduced in Glen, Heather (ed.), *The Cambridge Companion to the Brontës*, Cambridge University Press, 2002.

Booklist

Abbreviation: *PL* = Ruijssenaars, Eric, *Charlotte Brontë's Promised Land.*

Blyth D. 2004. *Brussels for Pleasure* (see Walk 6, Charlotte Brontë and the Royal Quarter). London: Pallas Athene.

Chadwick EH. 1914. *In the Footsteps of the Brontës.* London: Sir I. Pitman & Sons.

Cumberland G. 1911. Charlotte Brontë's street in Brussels today. *Cornhill Magazine.* [Reprinted in *PL*, pp. 84-6.]

Davies S. 1996. *Four Dreamers and Emily.* London: The Women's Press Ltd.

Gaskell E. 1857. *The Life of Charlotte Brontë.* London: Smith, Elder & Co.

Gérin W. 1967. *Charlotte Brontë: the Evolution of Genius.* Oxford: Oxford University Press.

Lonoff S. ed. 1997. *The Belgian Essays: a Critical Edition.* New Haven, CT: Yale University Press.

MacDonald F. 1914. *The Secret of Charlotte Brontë.* London: T.C. & E.C. Jack.

Ruijssenaars E. 2000. *Charlotte Brontë's Promised Land: The Pensionnat Heger and other Brontë places in Brussels.* Haworth: The Bronte Society.

Ruijssenaars E. 2003. *The Pensionnat Revisited: more light shed on the Brussels of the Brontës.* The Netherlands.

Spielmann MH. 1916. Charlotte Brontë in Brussels. *The Times Literary Supplement.* [Reprinted in *PL*, pp. 93-101.]

Spielmann MH. 1919. The Inner History of the Brontë-Heger letters. *Fortnightly Review* 111, pp. 599-605.

Smith M. ed. 1995. *The Letters of Charlotte Brontë.* Volume I, 1829-1847. Oxford: Clarendon Press.

Trafton A. 1871. A Visit to Charlotte Brontë's School in Brussels. *Scribner's Monthly.* 3:2. [Reprinted in *PL*, pp. 58-60.]

Index

There are constant references throughout the book to Charlotte and Emily Brontë, *Villette* and *The Professor*. These are therefore not listed in the index.

Helen MacEwan
(*photo: Cassandre Sturbois*)

Helen MacEwan, who conceived the idea of the Brussels Brontë Group, works in Brussels as a translator and has also taught English as a foreign language. Her passion for nineteenth-century literature dates back to reading *Jane Eyre* at the age of twelve. She wrote this book to share her experience of founding a literary association and her fascination with Charlotte and Emily Brontë's stay in Brussels.

The Brussels Brontë Group was founded in 2006 as a branch of the Brontë Society, with members in both Belgium and the Netherlands. It was the first ever branch of the Society in Brussels, where Charlotte and Emily Brontë lived in 1842-3, an experience which inspired two of Charlotte's four novels, *The Professor* and *Villette*. The sisters' stay in Brussels has always intrigued those interested in their lives and works and the group grew rapidly, its multinational membership testifying to the Brontës' appeal to readers worldwide. The group established the first regular guided Brontë walks in Brussels and organises a varied programme of events in the city.

www.thebrusselsbrontegroup.org
www.brusselsbronte.blogspot.com